YES, SOMETIMES IT IS ABOUT THE
MONEY

STEVE SCHULZ

ISBN 978-1-936677-32-0
Printed in the United States of America

This book is dedicated to those who have walked before me, blazing the trail to success; to those who have walked beside me, cheering me along the way; and to those who will walk behind me, learning from my mistakes and using the lessons to catapult them to success beyond their wildest dreams.

Contents

Acknowledgments

For many years I have been asked, encouraged and yelled at to tell my story. Now is the time. I wrote this book from my heart. I wrote it to let you know that if you really want to achieve something, it is possible. I have always surrounded myself with great people; people better than me. Never in life do we need to go it alone. If I ever end up back in a classroom, I will never give an individual test. Life is a group effort. There are many people in my life that I need to thank for making my life wonderful.

John and Barb Schulz: Thank you for the values that shaped who I am today.

Colleen Schulz: Thank you for your understanding when my dreams often butted heads with reality. You have kept me grounded but have allowed me to fly. I love you.

Megan, Emily and Mike: Thank you for putting up with me. But it's all been worth it right? I am so proud of you. You have unlimited potential and you prove it every day. I love you.

Jenn Kiely: You were the true inspiration to get this ball rolling. Thank you for encouraging me throughout this project.

Pat Hintze: You are the best. You continue to amaze me.

Jordan Adler: One of the greatest friends in my life. You inspire me every day.

Scott Pospichal: It's been a great ride my friend. Let's keep it going. I value our friendship.

Kenny Troutt: The gift you have given me and my family is priceless. Thank you for the Excel opportunity, your friendship and inspiration.

Steve Smith: You keep me in check. You always steered me in the right direction. Thank you for believing in me.

Bill Andreoli: When I was at my darkest hour, you were there. Thank you.

Jimmy Delmore: You have had a major positive impact on my life. Thank you for all of your words of wisdom.

Coach Kuhl: You are with me every day of my life. Thank you for your leadership.

Annie Trajlinek: One of my best friends on the planet. We will be in rocking chairs together.

Robert T. Buss: No words can describe the fun, the great memories and lasting friendship you have given me.

Melody Marler: Thank you for your valuable publishing advice and constant encouragement. On Wisconsin!

Vanessa Hunter: You are the only person who has read this book more often than I have. Your vision, creativity and dedication are invaluable to me.

Kody and Jodi Bateman: You are amazing. Thank you for believing in me. We will see a BILLION together!

Foreword

Steve Schulz is living proof that nice guys finish first. We have many mutual friends and virtually all of us would agree that Steve is one of the good guys. Have you ever looked down at the caller ID on your smart phone and noticed that it was someone you didn't want to talk to? In fact the person calling you was someone that was guaranteed to zap your energy for the rest of the day? What did you do? You pressed the "ignore" button on your phone! You knew from the second your phone rang that if you answered it you would get an earful of negativity that was sure to, at the very least, bum you out, and at the worst, mess up your entire day. Steve Schulz is the opposite of that. When you meet Steve you are energized by his friendly demeanor, his attitude toward life, and his spontaneous sense of humor. Everyone loves Steve.

And when it really comes down to it, one of the main reasons Steve has done well in business is because people want to be around him. He is easy to be with and he makes people feel good about themselves.

That is probably one of the reasons why we are friends today. I always look forward to seeing or talking with Steve. If Steve were to call me with a business idea, I would want to hear what he has to say because, first, I know he has my best interest in mind, and second, I like him. These are two of the critical keys to success in business.

I met Steve in the early 90s when we both signed up for the same network marketing company. We were both flat broke. I had dabbled in many companies over a period of 10 years but never made any money, and Steve had no experience in network marketing at all. In his words he was a "dead broke full-time school teacher!" We were both learning the ins and outs of network marketing and because Steve was a nice guy, I wanted to be around him. We instantly became good friends and over the next 10 years we both built sizable five-figure monthly incomes. As a result, we spent many hours training together and traveling all over the world. I remember sitting in a crowd of new distributors at an event listening to Steve and his business partner train. I don't remember exactly what they said but I do remember that they were fun, funny and yes, easy to like.

Why is this important? These are the same qualities that will make someone want to be around you and do business with you. It's a simple formula. Yes, it's true, this book IS about making money and sometimes it IS about the money. But you must become someone others want to be around if you want them to listen to you. When Steve approaches someone who knows him about a business, most of the time they say, "Sure, Steve — what have you got? Tell me more!" People want to know what Steve is up to because he's a likable guy and he's fun to be around. After all, someone who has been making a full-time living in this profession for more than 20 years must be doing something right!

Here's the bottom line: Steve brings credibility to our profession and he has proven that it is OK to be a nice guy and still have a wildly successful business. For some reason people in business think that to have it all, you must step on others. You must be shrewd, tenacious, and cutthroat! According to some business experts, you must be willing to climb over bodies to get to the top and you can only win at the expense of others. Steve's story isn't just compelling because he has won in life, but because he did it without hurting or exploiting others. He cares about people. One of the main reasons people like him is because his mission is to serve others and treat people right.

Since this book is about money, let's talk about money for a minute. To be perfectly honest, back in my early days of mac and cheese three times a week — at 33 cents a box — and taking the bus to work because I didn't have the money to fix my car, my number one need was to get money. I understood the idea of value exchange and knew that I needed to provide a lot of value to begin making money. But make no mistake about it, I got into network marketing to make money. Most people join because they want to have the freedom that a constant flow of income into their bank accounts can provide. If you were to ask 1,000 people to answer in one word why they got involved in network marketing, you would find that the highest percentage would say "money!" They wouldn't say "friends" or "travel" or "freedom," although all of these things are important. They want money because the money represents choices, regardless of what your life mission might be. I was no different and most likely neither are you! The green stuff is pretty powerful and compelling. It's one of the main reasons we get involved, and it's one of the key components to attracting others into our businesses. Steve nails it in this book. He does several things that make network marketing work for him, and you can do the same thing:

- Be likable.
- Be friendly.
- Have fun.
- Keep it simple.
- Explain the money.

Get out your highlighter and pen and mark up this book! Use it as a guidebook to making your fortune in network marketing. You're holding your future in your hands right now. See ya on the beach!

Jordan Adler
Network Marketing Millionaire
Author of the bestseller Beach Money®

Money: Why You Need It and How You Can Help People With It

My entire life I have heard people say, "Money is not everything," or, "Money brings out the evil in people." I have never understood that. I always thought the people who said that were the ones who didn't have any money! I believe that if you are a good person who has money, you will do good things. If you are a bad person who has money, well, you will continue to do bad things. This book is about money. How to get it, why you need it and how you can help a lot of people with it.

I grew up in the small town of Wisconsin Dells, in southcentral Wisconsin. It was a great place to grow up. It had everything — that small town feel but the action of a big city. Wisconsin Dells is the Midwest's number one tourist attraction. The Wisconsin River is the main attraction. For thousands of years, the Wisconsin River has carved out the beautiful sandstone cliffs that line this powerful hard-working river. A town of only 2,400 permanent residents plays host to more than 100,000 guests from all over the world on a daily basis from Memorial Day through Labor Day each year. Today, Wisconsin Dells is known as the water park capital of the world and has turned into a year-round tourist destination.

I realize now that growing up in "The Dells" shaped my way of thinking about money and dealing with people. I loved this town and still do. I remember Friday nights — the lights on the new football field, the packed stands and our love for the home team. It didn't matter what the sport was, the Chiefs were the only game in town. As a young boy, Friday night was special. My friends and I would go and watch our heroes on the field that we dreamed of playing on one day. When that day came, we made the most of it.

My football coach, Fred Kuhl was a man who shaped me — and hundreds like me — into the person I am today. I love that man. I have never heard a negative word about Coach Kuhl. He worked us hard but loved us deeply. During practice he would always tell us, "You will understand why we do this on Friday night. It will be worth it." Coach could always get the most out of his players. Just when we thought we were going to die, he was able to get a little more out of us and that made all of the difference on Friday night.

Coach said to me one time, "Never say, 'I wish I would have'." I will never forget that. I have lived my entire life with that statement in my head. With every decision I make, I hear Coach's words in my ears. It hasn't always worked out, but I have no regrets.

To paraphrase the famous quote by hockey legend Wayne Gretzky, remember, 100 percent of the shots you don't take don't go in. Take shots. Just take a shot. What if it works? Start living your life with that attitude and watch what happens. You will make more money, meet more people, and enjoy life to its fullest.

Wisconsin Dells offered so many opportunities. I was working 40 hours a week at age 12. Parking cars was my first summer job. Cars would stream into this huge parking lot full of people on their way to take a ride up the Wisconsin River on a Dells boat trip. My job was to say, "park there," and make sure people were actually there to take a Dells boat trip. As the summer dragged on, I started to add up the money the boat company was making. It seemed as though I parked thousands of cars filled with people willing to spend money — a lot of money — in our little town each day. I thought if I just had a boat I could cash in as well!

My other jobs included washing dishes, bussing tables, working the go-kart tracks, batting cages, water parks, cleaning hotel rooms, working the front desk at the hotel and selling liquor and, of course, cheese — it was Wisconsin!

My family did not have a lot of money. We were not poor by any means, but I never thought we were rich. My parents, John and Barb Schulz, are hard-working people, and they took great care of me, my brother and my two sisters. I definitely got my work ethic and my passion for wealth from my mother. She is an extremely hard worker. She often had two jobs, and she taught me the value of saving money. My mother and her sister, my Aunt Marilyn, ran a number of resorts in Wisconsin Dells. Aunt Marilyn handled the front desk operations while mom took care of the housekeeping duties. My mom got the wrong end of that deal! She was in charge of turning over hundreds of hotel rooms in just a few hours every day, and when her staff did not show up for work — you guessed it — mom cleaned the rooms. During the summer months, she NEVER took a day off. I watched her wear out three pairs of shoes per summer. I would often come in to help clean the rooms, carry luggage for our guests, and do yard work — anything to earn extra money. I knew my parents were not going to be able to pay for my college education, so, I had to make money and save it.

One summer I had three jobs. I literally got paid around the clock. I worked at a liquor store and a grocery store and did a graveyard shift at the resort. The latter was the best because the resort was always full; the front desk closed at 11 p.m. and I could go to sleep. I was basically there for emergencies. So, in essence, I got paid to sleep.

Wisconsin Dells and my mother certainly played a role in my entrepreneurial spirit. Big money is made in the Dells and the business owners often enjoyed nine months off because of their hard work during the summer months. I wanted to experience that. I was never afraid of hard work. I just did not have the vehicle to get me to where I needed to be. I was trading time for money and I knew that was not going to cut it.

Then I went to work for a guy that really changed my life — Jimmy Delmore. He owned a liquor store and a grocery story. Both businesses shared the same parking lot. Jimmy was 17 years older than me and played on my summer softball league team. And he was a player! He played younger than most guys on the team. He could hit, but mainly he could run. Jimmy was fast and could rundown any ball hit his way in the outfield. We had a great team. If we lost two games all summer long, that was a bad year.

On game days, Jimmy and I and some of our teammates would meet at the liquor store and talk strategy while we worked. We lived for Wednesday night softball, and hundreds of people would come to watch us play. We should have sold tickets. Not only was Jimmy good on the field, he was a GREAT businessman. His stores made money — lots of money. He was very organized and was able to negotiate great deals. I learned a lot from Jimmy. I learned that if you work hard and treat people right, you would be successful. I also learned that if I was ever going to make the kind of money Jimmy made, I needed to be the boss. Trading time for money was not the answer.

During my four and a half years of college, I was able to pay for my tuition, fees and books, without having to take out any student loans, thanks to my summer employment in Wisconsin Dells. Working 12-hour days, I could make enough in one summer to pay for a full year of school and still have some money left over. It was hard work, but earning enough money for college while working with my friends, meeting people from all over the country and forming lifelong relationships made it worth it.

I was always looking for ways to make extra money during my college years. I wasn't the best student so I didn't want to hold down a job during the school year. I needed that time to study. Well, that was an excuse. Maybe if I didn't have so much "fun" in college, I could have been a better student.

I attended the University of Wisconsin-La Crosse. My roommates and I had a great time. We could come up with any reason to have a party or go downtown. Happy hour with 10-cent taps was pretty inviting! I used to think, "How do these bar owners make any money?" They must have. They offered happy hour every night. I would count how many people were in the bar, guess how much each person spent and estimate the bar owner's overhead costs. Once again, I decided I needed to be the boss if I was going to make money.

During my junior year of college, my roommates and I decided we were smarter than the odds-makers in Las Vegas. We heard about a group of guys on campus who were placing bets on NFL games, and we thought we had found an easy way to make money. All we had to do was pick the teams based on the odds in *USA Today*. Simple right? Wrong!

We soon discovered that those hotels and casinos were not built by people who won. They were built by the girls and guys like me and my roommates who thought they could beat the system. My roommate "Louie" — I changed the name to protect the innocent — would take all of our bets and pass them on to one guy. I never knew who that guy was and I didn't really want to know. I think he lived in the shadows.

We had two weeks to bet on the games we wanted to, and then we had to pay up or collect. We had until Tuesday of the second week, after the Monday night football game, to do that. We figured if we lost over the weekend, we could make it all up on Monday night. Stupid thinking!

It's not like we lost money every week, but overall we lost. Things started to get crazy. We bet money on anything and every game we could. We went from NFL games to the NBA to MLB. We even had some guys betting on hockey games in the NHL. No one got hurt, but no one made any money either.

During my senior year, the guys wanted to start betting on games again. I thought to myself, "Why? The house always wins." I guess there is a reason why people get into trouble gambling. It's an addiction. I didn't think my roommates were addicted to gambling, but I didn't think they would win any money either.

Everyone became excited when the first week of the regular season in the NFL began. All of my roommates started looking at the odds and placing their bets. "Louie" called me into his room and explained to me that he had a plan. His plan was to keep the bets. Not pass them on to the guy from last year. He looked at me and said, "We can't lose." Famous last words. He asked me if I wanted to be in on it. Of course I did. I wasn't making any money the other way. "Louie" and I were best friends. We grew up together. We did everything together. If he was in, I was in.

After week one, "Louie" and I were down more than $800. I wanted to cry. I thought to myself, "I can't afford to lose." I have to pay for college. What did I get myself into? I told him, "I'm out! I can't do this." What was I thinking? All week long I wondered how I was going to be able to pay for this mess I had gotten into. It was a terrible week. I didn't sleep very much. My schoolwork suffered. I was a mess! I was out!

I went home to the Dells the following Friday to relax. OK, I went home so my mom could do my laundry and I could get some food. I tried not to think about the mess I had gotten myself into. I looked at it as a learning experience. Gambling was dangerous and I had learned my lesson.

When I got back to school on Sunday night, "Louie" called me into his room. He had a very thought-provoking look on his face. He just stared at me. I asked him what he was looking at. He simply asked me, "Are you in or are you out?" Before I had a chance to answer him he asked again, "Are you in or are you out?"

"Are you telling me you held the bets this weekend?" I asked. He replied, "Are you in or are you out?"

"If you're in, I'm in," I said.

"Good, because we're up $1,200," he said.

I couldn't believe it. Not only did we gain back the $800 we had lost, but we made another $1,200. And we never lost again. Every other Tuesday, we made money because the house does not lose. To this day, my roommates do not know "Louie" and I held the bets. If they knew, they never would have paid us. Ha!

We made a lot of money. The problem was I could not deposit it into the bank. We were spending it as fast as we made it. My parents would always ask me where I was getting the money to buy the televisions, VCRs, cameras and lots of clothes. I told them we were placing a few bets on games. My dad was a special agent with the Division of Criminal Investigation. He wasn't buying it. He talked to me one day just before I headed back to school.

He put his arm around me and said, "If you get caught placing a bet, it's like getting a parking ticket. If you get caught taking the bets, it's a felony. Have a nice week." He scared me to death! But not enough to stop! After my senior year, my buddies, roommates and best friends all went their separate ways. I'm still in touch with all of them. None of us have a gambling problem.

I learned a lot from that experience. I learned I needed to be the boss. I had to call the shots. The people who worked for others were pawns. They made the owners rich. They did all the work and the owners received the major benefits. I knew I needed to own my own business.

Now don't get me wrong. I didn't begrudge the business owners. They were the ones who took the chance to start their own business and they assumed the most risk. They understood how the game was played. The employees understood how the game was played as well. They each chose their role and accepted it.

The choice I made was to be on the owner's side of the spreadsheet. The problem was I didn't have enough money to open up a Kool-Aid stand. I knew I was going to do something; I just needed to figure out what.

"Louie," whose real name was Pat, had the same dream. We wanted to start a business together. We both knew that if we were going to make the kind of money we wanted to make, we had to be the boss.

After college, Pat took a sales position with a paper company in Milwaukee and I worked for the *Milwaukee Journal/Sentinel*. We talked almost every day. We played on the same softball team in the Milwaukee area. We talked about "someday" when we would own our own business.

What If It Works?

Four years after Pat and I graduated from college, we were still looking for the right opportunity. Pat would go to business expos and look at different franchising options and come back depressed. We couldn't afford to start anything. It cost millions of dollars just to get the logo rights from places like McDonald's, Burger King, and Wendy's. It was still hundreds of thousands of dollars for places like Dairy Queen, TCBY, and Pennzoil's garages.

We looked at starting a sporting goods store, but it was too expensive. We looked at opening a driving range, but we couldn't find the right location. We looked at buying a golf course, but we couldn't afford the first hole. We looked at miniature golf courses with batting cages and a concession stand and we got a little further with that idea. We had the perfect location; right off I-94 and Highway 83 in Delafield, Wisconsin. We knew thousands of people would drive by and see our operation. It was perfect! I was already spending the fortune we were going to make. I could see the bright lights, hear the music playing, see the lines of people waiting to get in, and smell the fresh popped popcorn, hot dogs, and cheese brats on the grill. We thought we had finally found what we had been looking for over the past 14 years. But there was one major problem. The land we needed for the project was priced at $3.4 million. We were $3,398,000 short.

We were right about one thing. The land was in a perfect location. I know that because today, Best Buy, Panera Bread, Verizon, Kohl's, Sports Authority, Five Guys, Cost Cutters, Sentry Foods, and about 15 other businesses share the land of my dreams! I still get depressed when I drive by.

We tried to get financing but no one — I mean no one — believed in our dream. Banks, our friends, not even our parents could see what we saw in this opportunity. We decided to move on and keep looking. We knew we could be successful — all we needed was a chance. Our drive, our work ethic and our will to win were not the issue. We just needed a break.

That break was on its way. Colleen and I were married on July 11, 1987. The temperature was 107 degrees. The wedding party was melting and so were our guests, but it was a wonderful day shared by our friends and family.

Two years later, our daughter Megan was born. Jan. 11, 1989 was a very special day. I felt like a kid on Christmas Day. Her bright red hair was the talk of the maternity ward. Everyone wanted to see our special child. God had blessed us with the greatest gift, a healthy little girl. I couldn't stop looking at her. I couldn't believe she was mine.

It wasn't until the hospital released Colleen and allowed us to take Megan home that we realized we had no idea how to take care of a newborn baby. We were clueless, but we grew up in a hurry. The responsibility was enormous but we were up to the challenge.

We purchased our first home in Milwaukee that same year. It was a small, 900-square-foot ranch on the south side. We paid $64,000 for the two-bedroom starter home and wondered how in the world we were going to pay for it. That was a ton of money. Colleen already had a teaching position. She taught first grade in Milwaukee. But even with her salary and my pay from the *Journal/Sentinel* combined, it seemed as though we always had more month than money. (You're likely shaking your head right now because you can relate.)

We weren't even living paycheck to paycheck. Colleen's parents would slip us $50 and buy us groceries every time they visited. I wanted them to come down more often. I delivered phone books to make extra money. I remember delivering 800 large Milwaukee phone books for $35. I also worked at County Stadium, home of the Milwaukee Brewers, making public address announcements. Colleen took part in diaper surveys so we could get free diapers.

We worked those crazy jobs because we needed to. We NEVER went out for dinner or to see a movie. We were struggling financially. We did what we needed to do to get by. Character building — that's what it was.

At the *Milwaukee Journal/Sentinel* I was responsible for 358 twelve-year-old boys and girls and their paper routes. When they decided it was too cold to do their routes, I received the phone calls and had to deliver the papers myself. I was a glorified paperboy. My full-time job was keeping the routes full. I never succeeded. I knew this was not for me. I needed to be the boss!

I still had not found what I was looking for. Colleen and I decided I could not continue to work the long hours I put in at the *Journal/Sentinel*. I went back to college to get my teaching certification. I thought having two teachers in the house would be a great thing. The money wasn't bad and the work schedule was great. It only took me three semesters to complete the coursework.

As soon as I graduated, I got a job teaching seventh grade English in Milwaukee. I had five classes, the smallest of which included 43 kids. I had to have two classrooms; the dividing door was opened up to accommodate all the students. I taught a total of 235 seventh graders throughout the day. But during parent teacher conferences, I only saw 23 parents. I'm not kidding! One parent yelled at me for her child's behavior. I stopped her and said, "He's with you 70 percent of the time. You tell me where the problem is." The kids were great. The parents needed a time out!

September 9, 1990, was a day that changed our lives forever. It was a Sunday that started out like any other Sunday, except my best friend Pat had some news that he had been keeping from me for a few days. Pat called me at 10:30 p.m. that Sunday night and asked me what I was doing.

I said, "I'm going to bed. Why, what do you want?"

He said, "Just wait. I'm coming over." And he hung up.

I turned to Colleen and said, "If it's important enough for Pat to call me at 10:30 at night, it must be important enough for me to listen to what he has to say."

Pat came over to my house and threw a piece of paper on my living room table and said, "Tell me why this won't work."

I looked at it for a few minutes and said, "Because it's one of those multi-level deals, that is why it won't work."

He just looked at me and smiled. He said, "How would you like to get paid every time someone made a long-distance phone call?" My first reaction was disbelief. I did not know of any company willing to pay others for getting long distance customers. Besides, everyone I knew already had long distance and probably with AT&T, the founder of the industry. How could we possibly compete with them?

Pat and I stared at the poor photocopy of the compensation plan for two hours. We tried to figure out how it worked and how the company could pay out all that money. After two hours, Colleen came out of our bedroom and said, "I've been listening to you guys for two hours. For $400 — what if it works?" She turned around and went back to bed, shutting the door behind her.

Pat and I stared at the closed door. We did not have an answer for Colleen. The reason we didn't have an answer for Colleen was because we were trying to find reasons why it WOULDN'T work instead of reasons why it WOULD work. That's the negative world we live in. Most people do what Pat and I did — they find reasons why the business won't work instead of reasons why it will.

The craziest part of the whole night was the fact that we had been looking for an opportunity like this since we were 12 years old. We were now 26. Fourteen years of looking and we didn't even see it. Colleen did!

We looked at each other and said, "Let's go!" We decided that it just might work. So what if it didn't? I only had to invest about $400. It was money we didn't have, but we needed to take the shot. This decision changed our lives, our children's lives and our future grandchildren's lives for generations to come.

Before we actually filled out the paperwork to get started, we checked the company out. We had to make sure it was right, it was ready, and it was real. We had some credibility and we wanted to keep it! We did not know the first thing about checking out a company. So the next day, I called in sick. Pat came over to my house around 8 a.m. and we went to Denny's restaurant to talk a little bit more about this opportunity. When we got to the restaurant we noticed there was a pay phone just outside the front door. We saw an 800 number on the bottom of the poor photocopy we had, so we dialed the number. A young woman answered, "Good morning, Excel Communications." We hung up and said, "They're real, let's go make some money."

I guess all I really wanted to know was that someone was there to take our money. I wasn't concerned about how long they had been in business. I didn't care that we could only do business in 23 states. It didn't bother me that the home office was only 900 square feet. All I knew were the numbers on the compensation plan that I had and if they paid according to the plan, I was going to make money. Lots of money!

Later that morning we called our sponsor, Mike, and asked if we could meet him for lunch because we had a few questions. He is the man directly responsible for changing the financial direction of my life, and we are still friends today. We met Mike for lunch and started asking questions. We asked Mike if he had gotten a check from Excel. He said, "No, I haven't gotten a check yet." We said, "That's OK, you're just getting started. Do you know of anyone who has gotten a check from Excel?" He paused and said, "No, I don't know of anyone who has actually gotten a check. We said, "That's fine."

We asked Mike how the phone service was. Was it crackly? Was it just like AT&T, MCI or Sprint? Mike looked at us and said, "I'm not quite on the service yet." Now we're starting to figure this out a bit. I said, "Mike, do you know anyone who is using Excel's service today?"

He looked down and said, "No, I don't know anyone." Pat said, "Don't worry about it. We're going to do it anyway." Mike said, "You are? Well, me too then!" He wasn't even in yet!

I know this happened because he told us later. He called his sponsor, a buddy of his from Green Bay and said, "Hey, we have a couple of 'live ones' in Milwaukee. We better get in this thing just in case they decide to do something with it." That was a pretty good idea on Mike's part. From that day forward, it was an unbelievable journey.

Our daughter Emily was born 22 months after Megan. On Sept. 29, 1990, our second little miracle became part of the family. With her blonde hair and blue eyes I knew lots of hearts were going to be broken. I was right! She was perfect. She even had those crooked little fingers like me, like her grandmother, and like her great-grandmother.

Megan and Emily shared everything, including the second bedroom in our little house. Poor Emily never got anything new. She got hand-me-down clothes, toys, everything. She didn't care. She had all the love she needed from me, Colleen, and her big sister, Megan.

We had great neighbors who loved the girls as their own. Jim was retired and often had Megan in his garage sorting out nuts and bolts. He made a little stool for her to stand on while she did her work. She took it very seriously. While Megan was sorting nuts and bolts, Emily was at Andy and Mae's front door asking for cookies. Shyness was something Emily lacked. She always came home with the goods and yes, she even shared with her big sister after her hard day's work.

Colleen could not bear the thought of leaving the girls at daycare while we both worked. So, she quit her teaching job when Emily was born. The goal was to have her go back to work when Emily was in school. It never happened. Colleen has not worked another day for someone else since.

Special Relationship

Pat Hintze and I have been friends since we were eight years old. We went through elementary school together. We were best friends in high school and we were college roommates. There is no doubt that we know each other better than our wives do and that will always be the case. When I got married, Colleen knew Pat was part of the package.

Growing up in Wisconsin Dells gave Pat the same drive for money that I had. Pat worked at a very young age doing all sorts of crazy summer jobs. He worked throughout the school year at a local restaurant. Pat was the best short-order cook you could find.

Growing up with Pat was amazing. We always had fun together, whether we went to Lambeau Field to watch the Green Bay Packers play, went fishing, played sports or just sat around the house. Pat taught me how to play golf. He was also the source of a lot of my frustration as I learned that stupid game! But I would always come back for more. In golf, it's that one good shot that keeps you coming back. I would always say, "If I could just hit the ball like that every time, I'd be on the PGA Tour."

Golf, like life, is a humbling game. People who don't play golf have no idea how good Phil Mickelson or any PGA pro is. These men and women not only have the talent, but they have the head game that goes with it. That was Pat. Nothing seemed to bother him. He was never rattled. The more pressure he felt, the better he performed.

There was a group of eight guys that Pat and I took to Myrtle Beach every March to play golf. This was the highlight of our year. These eight guys were family — four against four. Team Tiger Woods versus Team Freddie Couples. We called it the Rider-less Cup! It was five days of intense competition for nothing more than bragging rights for the rest of the year.

I cannot tell you how many times it came down to Pat having to make a 40-foot putt to win the match, and he would always put it in the bottom of the cup. Pat was not on my team and I had to witness that type of play over, and over, and over again. That guy was clutch and it wasn't just on the golf course. He would hit the big shot during a high school basketball game, hit the big home run to win a softball game, and make an unbelievable play at shortstop to end the inning. I was a fan. I loved to watch that guy play.

One day, we were just sitting in his yard trying to find something to do when he picked up his new bow. For some reason at age 12, we thought it would be a great idea to shoot the bow straight up into the air. The second the arrow cleared the bow; we knew we were in trouble. Remembering what Mr. Felt taught us in seventh grade science — what goes up, must come down — we ran for our lives!

We hid under the awning along the side of his house and prayed. It seemed like a lifetime before we heard the thud. We both stood there in utter amazement when we realized the arrow that had traveled to the moon and back was now stuck in the hood of the new Ford Pinto belonging to Pat's dad.

Obviously, the world had just come to an end. We were as good as dead. We didn't know how in the world we were going to explain that one. There was no way out. We couldn't blame it on Pat's little brother Mike because he was too small to pull the bow back. So we did the next best thing — nothing.

We didn't say a word. We were determined to take our little secret to the grave. Pat's dad had no idea how the dent, which looked like a bullet hole, ended up in the hood of his new car. We both seemed just as puzzled. Pat's dad never did suspect that we had anything to do with it. I think it was 20 years later that we actually fessed up to the truth. The statute of limitations had run out so we thought we were safe. We all had a good laugh.

Pat and I would play little games and set goals. For instance, we had to catch 100 punts in a row or hit a tennis ball back and forth 50 times without hitting the ground. We would be outside for hours until we met our goal. To this day, I believe we always hit our goal. That was a sense of pride for us. We both live our lives the same way today. That sense of pride and willingness to win led us to the Excel Opportunity.

Rough Start

Our little house was now getting small. As the girls got older, we accumulated a lot of stuff. We needed more space. We put our little 900-square-foot house on the market and sold it in less than 30 days. We had lived in that house for about five years, and we made roughly $10,000 on the sale. I was excited!

We found a three-bedroom home with a great kitchen, dining room and family room in West Allis, Wisconsin, a western suburb of Milwaukee. The house was built in the 1950's and only had one bathroom, but it was perfect for us. Thanks to the money we made on the sale of our old house, our payments were a little bit less on our new home.

We lived on the back straightaway at the Milwaukee Mile, located at the state fairgrounds. On race day, you couldn't hear yourself think. Naps were out of the question. From Indy cars to NASCAR to concerts, there was always something going on. The house wasn't in the greatest neighborhood, but we made it our home.

My first goal in my new network marketing business with Excel was to make enough money to make our car payment. I remember Colleen saying, "If we could just get a free car out of this thing, that would be great."

I was excited about the opportunity, but I never really thought it would replace my teaching income. I thought it would be a great supplement, something I could do in my spare time and especially in the summer. After all, I was a college graduate with a double degree in elementary education and sociology. That's what I was planning to do for the rest of my life. I'd spent a lot time and money on my education and I couldn't just waste it, right?

I was already setting myself up for failure. What I was really saying was that it was no big deal if it didn't work out. I was already set with my great teaching position. My total investment was around $500 after I bought my business cards, a few brochures and some sign-up forms. Remember, there was no such thing as the Internet, as we know it today, back in 1990. Our business model used paper applications for customers and representatives and the US Postal Service.

I was completely clueless about how to build this business. I had no idea where to start, and wasn't even sure what the product or service was. I had no idea how much it cost or how customers were even gathered. The only thing I knew was that if I could get people to try the service, I was going to get paid. Then if I could show others how to do the same, I was going to get paid for their customers as well. Cool concept — if it worked.

I found a few other people in the Milwaukee area that had signed up to be reps and they were holding training classes by appointment. Pat and I thought we better go find out what we didn't know about this business and see if we could put some type of plan together.

We met with a young lady who was very nice and excited about the business. She was a trainer for the company, so we thought we were in good hands. Pat and I and one other person attended the training that was held in a small apartment in Brookfield, Wisconsin. We soon found out that the woman knew a fraction more about the business than we did. To qualify as a "trainer," all you needed to do was write a check.

Pat and I quickly realized we needed to be the trainers in the area. We were going to figure this business out and teach everyone else how it all worked. As a trainer, you got paid to teach and train other independent representatives, regardless of whether they were in your group or not. This was very exciting to us. We didn't know that was part of the deal when we joined.

We made plans to have a training center where we could hold weekly business presentations and trainings. This was a classic example of putting the cart before the horse. How were we going to pay for a training center? Who were we going to train? It cost an additional $295 to become a trainer. I didn't have the money.

Our first goal was to get some customers and a few reps. We got our phones set up on the service — I mean we sent the card in requesting that our long distance be changed over to Excel. I dropped the long distance request cards in a mailbox and thought, "What now?"

How will I know when our service will be active? Will there be any disruption in service? Who will I get my bill from? What if AT&T calls me about the switch? My simple business just got complicated.

I called customer service and, when he wasn't at lunch, he was able to answer my questions. I'm not kidding. I think there was one guy named Steve who WAS customer service. I called rep services and Steve answered that phone too!

I decided to have faith in the system. After all, Excel would not be in business if they couldn't sign up customers, right? I needed to believe that or I was dead in the water. Blind faith is all I had. Remember, my sponsor didn't know one person who was using the service.

I knew the process was underway because 30 days later I got a call from AT&T. They offered me $100 on the spot to come back. I wondered how in the world I was going to compete with that. I couldn't offer my customers $100 to sign up with me. That was crazy!

I immediately called my mom and dad and asked if they got a call from AT&T about switching back. My mom said she did. I asked her if she was offered any money. Mom said, "Yes, $100." I asked, "Did you switch back?"

My mother's answer put me at ease and made me realize I could compete with that 800-pound gorilla called AT&T. My mom said, "You mean more to me than $100. If I was that important to AT&T they should have given me the $100 years ago. No, I did not switch back."

That was music to my ears. I was going to get paid every time my parents made a long distance phone call. (Think about that!) I became determined to find thousands of people who thought the same way as my parents did. Customers and reps, that's what I needed. I made a list of people that I wanted to show the business to. I was starting to build my army so I could get paid for their customers as well.

I made a list that included my "can't miss prospects." These were the people who I knew were going to sign up — the people who were going to join simply because of our relationship. These were the people who would do anything I asked them to, especially if it involved making money. I was going to practice my presentation on these people because it did not really matter. They were in! This was the group of eight that I was going to build my empire around. I wanted to get these people out of the way first, and then tackle everyone else later.

I learned a major lesson: **"Believe in everyone, count on no one."** The first eight people that I showed the business to said I was crazy, said, 'Don't quit your day job." My brother-in-law laughed at me, but by doing so, absolutely sealed my success in this business. There was no way I was going to let my brother-in-law, Brian, say to me, "See, I knew that wasn't going to work. Why don't you go back to your real job?"

I didn't know much about the company, but I knew myself. So, the only way this wasn't going to work was if the company failed me. I was not afraid of hard work. I knew I just had to out-work everyone else and everything would take care of itself. The greatest revenge is massive success, and I would show Brian how wrong he was.

Well, three years after I showed Brian the business, he called. You need to understand something: He rarely called. I saw Brian nine times in that three-year period — at Christmas, Easter, and Thanksgiving — and we never talked about my new business. So when he called and wanted to talk to me, rather than his sister, I thought something was wrong. I said, "Brian, what's wrong?" He said, "I've been thinking ...."

I thought to myself, "I'm going to have so much fun with this." I said, "Yeah?" He said, "I've been thinking and I think it's time I get started with your business."

I just smiled and said, "Brian, what makes you think I'm going to let you in?"

He said, "What do you mean?"

I said, "Brian, I showed you this business three years ago. Why is it such a good deal today as opposed to three ago?"

Brian said, "Well, I saw you and Colleen quit your jobs. You bought a new house. You bought two new cars."

I said, "That's all true, but we have all the representatives we need in your area."

In truth, there wasn't a single Excel rep within a five county radius of his home. I just played with him, and continued to play with him, and after about 20 minutes, I said, "OK, I'll see what I can do."

After three years, Brian joined my business. He never went full-time but he was able to make some extra money on the side of his regular job. This is a lesson in persistence. If I had stopped working my business, would I ever have had the chance to get Brian in? No! I believe you will get everyone you talk to, eventually.

Another one of my original eight prospects was my sister, Robin. She is three years older than me. She has always been a self-starter, and she thinks very similar to the way I think about business. She has owned her own business for years. But I have also watched her struggle financially for years. Working hard has never been the issue for Robin. She works extremely hard. Sometimes, though, she needs to work smarter rather than harder — a lesson we can all learn.

I thought Robin would be perfect for this business. She actually was the first name I wrote down on my prospect list.

Robin was an on-air radio personality in a little town in east central Illinois called Hoopeston, a farming community with a population of about 7,000. It wasn't that Robin knew a lot of people, but everyone knew her. She was a bit of a celebrity in little ole Hoopeston. Robin and her husband Brian owned a landscape company, a resale shop and a small diner, and they and plowed snow in the winter.

I asked Robin how business was going one day in the summer of 1990, and she said it never rained, so they didn't have any lawns to cut. In the winter, she said it never snowed so their snow plowing business was just as bad. I thought to myself, "Robin, you need to move. It's a good thing people need to eat!"

Robin liked money. She was a very hard worker. She was not afraid to take a chance. She owned multiple businesses. She was the perfect prospect for my business, number one on my list. She was in for sure. I couldn't miss with that one. She loved me!

I drove four hours one-way to show her the business. Everything I said was positive, but she had a negative response. I could not believe what I was hearing. Making money every time someone made a phone call, how simple was that? She didn't get it. She even said to me that she didn't know anyone who made long distance phone calls. What?

Not only would my sister, my number one prospect, not become a representative in my business, she would not even try the service and become a customer.

I thought to myself, "OK."

To my sister, I said, "I'm not asking you to do anything different than what you are doing right now. You pick up the phone, dial one plus the area code, and make the call. Nothing changes! You will even get your bill the same way you get it today. The only difference is you will save money on something you use every day."

She wouldn't do it. I was sick. I wondered what I had gotten myself into. If I couldn't get her into the business, I couldn't get anyone. I drove back to Milwaukee hating the business. I couldn't believe I had gotten suckered into it. I drove directly over to Pat's house. I walked into his office, threw a blank rep and customer application on his desk and said, "This isn't going to work."

Pat said, "What do you mean?"

I said, "How am I supposed to get people that I don't even know, if I can't even sign up my sister as a customer?"

He said, "So what?" I said, "What do you mean so what?" He said, "Who are you going to sign up today?"

I said, "I'm not going to sign up anyone today. I'm going to 'take my ball and go home'."

Pat just looked at me, flicked a pen on his desk, and said, "You know Beave (my nickname), there is no way this company is going to pay us $30, $40, $50 or $100,000 a month if it's going to be lie-down easy."

I will never forget that. I found out that day that your best friends are going to beat you up in this business. Your family members are going to give you a hard time. They have a license to do that. These people know you too well.

I showed the business to my aunts, my uncles, my brother and both of my sisters, my parents and Colleen's parents. My parents were the only ones to at least try the service. In defense of Colleen's parents, they would have, but they were in a non-coverage area.

Some of these family members have struggled financially their entire lives and when presented with a possible solution, they said, "No." They ALL said no; no to becoming a representative and no to saving money on their phone service. I guess I could understand it if they didn't have phone service, but they did. They all did. What I also learned, looking back, is that every bit of broken glass and barbed wire you have to crawl over to get to where you want to be in this business, is worth it!

I told Colleen what happened with my sister and she told me to quit. Building the business would have been so much easier if I could have shown Colleen the end at the beginning. You see, I know how tough this business is to build with an unsupportive spouse. Colleen was the one who got us started, but her support and enthusiasm faded quickly.

I remember coming home one night after a business presentation and Colleen meeting me at the door. She said to me, "Why do you still do that stupid phone thing? We're not making any money."

I said, "Just wait. We don't have the right people yet. I have seen people who make more in a month than we make in a year. These people are far less talented than me. The only thing they have on us is time. Just wait, just wait, just wait!"

Imagine me telling Colleen up front that someday we would live in a 13,000-square-foot home that included five bedrooms, two gourmet kitchens, a theater room that seats 16, an exercise room, an office, a dining room, a sun room, a family room with 20-foot ceilings, a six-car garage, a pool nicer than any of those at hotels in the Milwaukee area, and a basketball court that the entire neighborhood would want to play on.

Imagine me telling her up front that we would have the free time to do whatever we wanted to — that I would never have to miss my children's sporting events, plays, or concerts. We would be able to take a vacation every year and not worry about the cost. We would be able to help our friends and family with whatever they needed. We would be able to enjoy the kind of freedom that we always dreamed about.

Imagine me telling her up front that we would have the kids' college education paid for before they reached junior high, and she would have the lake home we always wished we could afford.

But to achieve all of this, I needed to do a business presentation every Monday through Thursday. It would only take about an hour each night. Yeah, I needed to work nights because most people worked during the day and I needed to meet with them after work. I also needed to conduct a training class for a few hours on Saturday mornings and spend a few hours on the phone each day setting up appointments. I needed to work about 20 hours a week and travel a few times a year to the national convention and some regional rallies.

It took Colleen a bit longer to see the big picture. I would go to events and meet people who had the same vision that I had. Colleen did not attend those events because the children were so young and she was not able to share in the excitement. Today, all of that has changed.

Do you know what Colleen says to me now when I happen to be home on a particular night? "Don't you have a meeting to go to?" I laugh about it now, but at the time it was very difficult.

Looking For The Secret

I attended my first national convention about a month after I got started. When I was introduced to the top income-earners, I thought, "These people have nothing on me. If they can do it, I can do it!" These people were just like me. They came from all walks of life. Some were schoolteachers. Some were in sales. Some were stay-at-home moms and dads. Some owned their own businesses. Everyone was different but they all had the same goal. They all wanted to create a better life for themselves and their families. I fit in perfectly. I also wanted to create a better life for myself and for my family. All I needed to do was the work.

Pat and I had worked the business hard for 90 days. We set up some hotel meetings. We did a lot of home business presentations. We talked to a lot of people who said they were in. We planted a lot of seeds. It was just a matter of time until we would see this little business of ours take off.

I got a call from Pat while I was at work one day. He said that our downline report had just arrived in the mail. Now remember, we did not have the Internet to track our downline on a daily basis. Our first commission check was included in this report. We got paid 90 days in arrears. I told Pat not to open it — I would be right over.

That was a huge day for us. We were about to see the fruits of our labor; 90 days of working the business was about to pay off. I was shaking. I could not drive over to Pat's house fast enough. It was like I had just won the lottery and I was cashing in the winning ticket. Everything that I hoped for was about to become a reality. I was able to start my own business. I was the boss. I called the shots. It was perfect!

When I got to Pat's house, I saw the envelope that contained my future. I opened it very carefully. We both saw the printout and we both saw the check — our first check! It was for 46 cents. Pat and I looked at each other and almost in stereo said, "Yes!" We knew at that point that the system was in place. Everything Excel said they were going to do, they did! We saw the activity on our report and it matched the amount of the check.

The only thing wrong with this scenario was that the printout wasn't big enough. From that day forward, the only thing I wanted to do was increase the pages of our printout. I knew that if the pages of the printout increased, a larger check had to follow. I knew exactly what I needed to do. I needed to build an army of people doing and thinking the exact same things I did. Simple, right? **It did not take me very long to realize that people did not think the way I thought.**

From my perspective, I wondered, "Who in their right mind doesn't want to have time freedom? Who would not want to become financially independent? Who wouldn't be willing to work 20 hours a week for the next five years to not have to do a blasted thing for the rest of their life?"

The answer is that almost everyone wants those things, but few are actually willing to take the risk and do the work. That's the reality of this business.

It's not that people are lazy; it's just that they can't see themselves doing what it takes to become successful. They are not willing to work all day at a JOB (which stands for Just Over Broke or Jerked Outta Bed) and then drive two to three hours to show someone, or a group of people, a business opportunity. They are not willing to work all week and give up a precious Saturday morning to teach others how to build a business on the side.

I think the main reason people feel this way is a fault of society. Most of us were taught that we need to go to school and get a diploma, then go to college and get a degree, then go work for someone for the next 40 to 50 years.

That's what my parents taught me. That is exactly what they said to me, and that's what I did. I got a great job as a teacher. I had job security as a male elementary school teacher. The kids loved me and I loved them. The problem was, I had grown up in an environment where I had learned that I needed to be the boss. Teaching school was just a stepping-stone in my life's work.

I will never forget when I decided to quit my teaching position to do this business full-time. My parents freaked out!

My mom said, "Don't you want to work hard and climb the corporate ladder?" I replied, "Wouldn't it be better if I actually owned the ladder?" When I left my teaching position, my grandmother said to me, "What about your benefits?" I told her that I could buy my benefits and be the boss. Needless to say, she did not understand. Very few people understood my way of thinking.

It actually took me almost three years of building before I quit my teaching job. And let me tell you, we struggled, and struggled, and struggled. It took us a very long time to get anything started in our business. We were excited, but we just couldn't get others to feel the same sense of excitement.

Someone told us once that if we were struggling, we needed to go to a meeting. Well, the closest meeting we could find to Milwaukee, Wisconsin, was Lexington, Kentucky. Pat and I knew there was going to be a big regional rally in Lexington and the top income-earner was going to be there. Now if anyone knew how to build this business, it had to be the top income-earner, right?

We drove eight and a half hours one way, intent on finding "the secret" to building this business. We arrived early and cornered the top income-earner. We started asking Paul our burning questions: How do you do this? How do you do that? How did you get your organization to where it is today? What are you doing to make your business explode?

His answer was a bit surprising. He said, "I really didn't do it. I just have a lot of good people in my group; they actually did it. You should go ask them." So we did. We asked them the same questions and got the same answers. They said, "We really didn't do it. We just have a lot of good people in our group. You should go ask them."

So we did. But guess what? They said the same thing.

Pat and I drove away from Lexington with the conclusion that *no one* actually does this business. It's just something you give away to other people. So we went back to

Milwaukee to find some people to *give it away to*. And guess what? That was doing it.

From that day forward, we started looking for people to simply give the business to. We wanted to find people who were better than we were and get out of the way. It worked!

The law of large numbers will rescue the persistent. We kept trying long enough to eventually find others we could give the business to, people who knew what they were doing. They were actually making their organizations grow. We got excited and starting exalting them, telling everyone about their success. Then they found others to give it away to, who were having more success than they were. It was incredible!

We started pointing to their success and other people got inspired by what they were hearing and seeing. Over the first three and a half years, all we managed to do was stumble across a few others to whom we gave the opportunity, and they were able to do the same. We got the chance to stand up in front of many people and take credit for it, but really, we didn't do it!

I guess the real secret to building a MLM business is to just sort people out. I look at the business today like a piece of art. It's not my job to get people to like my artwork; it's my job to get people to the museum and parade them past the exhibit, the business presentation. I let them stare at it for 20 or 30 minutes and then they can decide if they like it or not. It's not my job to talk anyone into the business. I found out early on that I could talk a lot of people into working the business, but they basically said "yes" just to get me off their back. They would stop returning my phone calls and quit within the week. Who needed that headache? I didn't and neither did they.

I also learned that if you try to drag someone across the finish line of success, it would never work. It will only bring you down. My friend Les Brown once said, "A man convinced against his will is of the same opinion still." I love that! After I realized this philosophy, the business became pretty easy.

I used to feel bad about bringing people into the business as I watched them struggle. But I soon realized that the reason they were struggling was because they didn't want to do it. I wanted success for them more then they wanted it for themselves. That's like you sponsoring me in the business because you are more dissatisfied with my life than I am. It will never work! I have to want to make a change in my life before any change will occur. It has nothing to do with you or the opportunity.

The secret is really just getting as many people in front of the opportunity as you possibly can. It is not your job to decide who's in and who's out. It's your job to show people the business opportunity. Get excited, have a simple presentation, and ask people to join your group. Do that over, and over, and over. I was starting to develop the attitude of. SW-SW-SW-SW: Some Will. Some Won't. So What. Some Waiting.

The only way you fail is if you quit showing the business. The one thing Pat and I absolutely did right is that we never quit. Today, I close all of my training classes by telling the group to be here one year from today. If you are here one year from today, you know good things are happening.

You Will Pay a Price

Most people think you pay a price for success. You don't. You pay a price for failure. The price I would have paid by not getting involved in network marketing was being a dead-broke teacher for the next 40 years. To me, it made sense to hold down a "real job" while building my business over three to five years if I did not have to do a blasted thing for the rest of my life! Most people are not willing to pay that price. They would rather complain about their job, talk about the people they work with, hate their boss, and not make the money they feel they deserve.

That probably is the most frustrating part of this business. You show someone a way to better their life, offer them a way to make more money, spend more time with the ones they love the most and travel the world. And they just don't get it. I've learned over the years that it's not that they don't see it — they are afraid they can't accomplish it. The fear of failure holds them back. They would rather not try at all than fail. It doesn't matter how simple the business is or what you say, some people will have that fear of failure. It's not your fault! Get over the fact that not everyone will join your business. It's not you — it's them.

I had a tough time understanding that in the beginning. I took the "no's" personally. I used to think, "What is wrong with me? Why don't these people see what I see? What am I missing?" Well, I wasn't missing anything. The people I was talking to had a fear of failure. They were comfortable in their everyday life. They had a routine. They had a comfort zone. They were not necessarily happy with their job, or with the money they were making, but they were not willing to do anything about it either.

Everything we have is tucked up nice and neat inside our comfort zone. Everything we want is outside our comfort zone. To paraphrase a famous quote, if you want something you don't currently have, you must do something different in your life to get it. I'm not talking about a new shirt. If you don't have time freedom, if you are not living in your dream home, if you are not driving your dream car, if you are not sending the right amount of money to your favorite church or charity, if you don't have your kids' college education already paid for, you need to do something different in your life. In order to do this, you need to step out of your comfort zone. It can be a bit painful for a while, but it will soon become your new comfort zone. When you step out of your comfort zone, you are doing something that you don't normally do because you are trying to achieve something you don't have today.

Remember the definition of insanity is doing the same thing over and over again, but expecting a different outcome. Look at your life today. Really look at it. Are you where you want to be financially? Are you living in your dream home or driving your dream car? Do you have the time or financial freedom you need?

Be honest. I know you may be saying — or yelling at me right now — that you do have everything in life that you need. Listen, there is nothing wrong with driving a ten-year-old Toyota Camry if you want to drive a ten-year-old Toyota Camry. All I'm saying is that if you want to drive a Lexus, but you have driven a Toyota Camry your entire life, you need to do something different. And to do that, you need to step out of your comfort zone. It's awkward, I know. But if you have a plan and understand what can happen when you execute your plan, the awkwardness goes away.

When I started in this profession, it was painful. I hated the fact that I had to "invite" my friends to look at my business and then try to "convince them" to join. I hated that part. But I loved the fact that I was going to make more money, I was going to be the boss, I was going to call the shots, and I was going to have time and financial freedom. You know you've made it when you get that awkward feeling when you are not building your business.

Once we could afford it, every year Colleen and I would take the kids to Florida, or Mexico, or the Dominican Republic, for at least a week. The week was awkward for me because I wasn't doing any business presentations, or trainings or conference calls.

When you decide to step out of your comfort zone, things will start changing in your life. You just need to understand there is a process. Once you understand that it will not happen overnight, everything will be fine. Slow and steady wins the race.

I know this all sounds simple, but it's not. This business can be depressing if you let it. Pat and I would travel from one event to another, and we would meet a lot of people and try to take what was working for them and apply it our business. But after each event, we would just get more depressed.

When you go to a national convention, a regional conference or even a super Saturday event, it seems like you see many people being paraded across the stage who have become super successful almost overnight. We would watch rep after rep receive awards, give great motivating speeches and tell us, "You can do it!"

We would see reps who got promoted to various levels in no time at all. They would stand on the stage and say, "I got promoted to senior executive in two and a half minutes!" Others would say, "We got promoted to vice chairman in a week and a half!" And still others would say, "I should be a Star Trek Commander by next Thursday!" We would listen to this all weekend long and then say to ourselves, "What's wrong with us? Why can't we be like those people? We stink at this business!" We would come away from those events with a severe case of, "What's wrong with me?"

It's very easy to get depressed in this business. To get depressed, all you need to do is compare your success to the success of others. If you are not at the top level of your company, you can get depressed. Even if you are at the top, the owners of the company make more than you. How depressing is that?

What I'm really trying to say is don't compare your success to the success of others. Compare your success to the goals you set for yourself. Set a goal, reach it, and then set another one. Continue this process and you will never get depressed because it's not about the people who walk across the stage; it's all about you and why you are working your business.

The only person you need to satisfy, impress or motivate is you. Set realistic goals and get after them!

You Will Be Inspired

You will meet some great people in this business. I loved the national conventions. I loved to see people walking across the stage receiving checks, monthly checks for more than I made in a year. That gave me hope. I remember saying, "If they can do it, I can do it."

All of these people had one thing in common; they all liked to help people. In network marketing, the only way you get to where you want to be is by helping others get to where they want to be. All the top income-earners understand this concept.

One person who instantly comes to mind is Jordan Adler. He is at the top of this profession, and makes twice as much monthly than the top 1 percent of the American population makes yearly. What makes Jordan so special is the way he treats people. When you spend time with him, you just feel better. He has a way of letting you know that you are somebody very special and success is coming your way. Jordan's smile and personality are contagious. You can't help but become a better person with him in your life.

Jordan got started in Excel Telecommunications about the same time we did. He struggled just like we did. We would see each other at national events and compare notes, share ideas and pull for each other's success. Looking back today, all we both really did was stick around long enough to get some good people in our group.

Today Jordan lives a lifestyle that most people can't even dream of. He has a number of homes across the country. He goes on exotic vacations to islands and countries I have never even heard of, whenever he wants to. He drives beautiful cars. He is a glider pilot and recently became a helicopter pilot. But Jordan has never forgotten where he came from. He loves his family and friends and understands his success came from helping others succeed. We've learned a lot from Jordan, but most of all, he's taught us to be persistent.

When my sister Angie, who lives in the Phoenix area, was getting married, she invited the family out for the ceremony. Jordan, who still has a home in Phoenix, asked me if we needed a ride from the airport to our hotel. I told him we did and that there would be 10 of us.

He said, "No problem, I will send my limo over to get you guys." On the plane flying to Phoenix, my cousin Heidi asked how we were going to get from the airport to the hotel. I told her my friend Jordan had a limo and his driver was picking us up. She looked at me, puzzled, and said, "He has a limo?" I replied, "Yes, he has a limo."

She said, "You mean he owns a limo service and is sending a car?" I said, "No, he does not own a limousine service. He has his own limo and driver."

Heidi was one of those family members who felt she had a license to beat me up. She was a customer I wished I had never signed up. She signed up reluctantly and I knew that if anything went wrong, I would hear about it for the rest of my life. Nothing went wrong, but she constantly told me how bad the service was even though she was saving money each month. She was having a difficult time grasping the success we were having with our business. She could not admit to herself the kind of money Jordan or I were making.

While standing at baggage claim at the Phoenix International Airport, she would not let up. She looked at me again and said, "Who has a limo? Does he go to the grocery store in his limo? Nobody does that." I smiled and said, "Jordan does."

She started complaining about the phone service right there at baggage claim. I calmly took $5 out of my pocket and threw it at her. I told her to switch back to AT&T. She said, "It will cost $10." I knew it didn't, but I threw down another $5 anyway. She found alternative transportation to the hotel. Needless to say, Heidi is not my customer or a rep in my business today.

I have met thousands of people from all walks of life — doctors, lawyers, teachers, salespeople, farmers, homemakers, CEOs and everyone in between. These people had the same dream as I had. The problem was only 20 percent of them would see the job through.

The 80/20 rule applies in life. Twenty percent of the people do 80 percent of the work. The 80/20 rule means that if you have 10 people in your group, two of them will be working, and you may be one of the two. The 80/20 rule means that if you have 100 people in your group, 80 of them won't do anything. The 80/20 rule means that if you have 1000 people in your group, 800 of them are going to quit! But you don't concentrate on the 800. If you concentrate on the 800, you could become suicidal. You need to concentrate on the 200. How would you like to have 200 people in your group at least trying?

I had a difficult time with the 80/20 rule until I understood how it worked. I often found myself wanting more success for my reps than they wanted for themselves. That philosophy never worked.

Back then, I had to find out where people were at in their lives. When I brought new people into the business, the first thing I asked them was, "Why are you doing this?" I needed to know where their head was. I used those reasons to remind them of why they were doing this when things got tough.

It didn't really matter though. I couldn't change the numbers. Only 20 percent of the people did the work despite their goals. I soon realized that all I needed to do was sort those people out. It wasn't my job to change them. I just needed to know who to work with. I attached myself to the 20 percenters.

I found out that you don't need a lot of people to make millions of dollars; you just need a few of the right ones. Now don't get me wrong, those in the 80 percenters group have value. They use the products or service, which generates income for you. But don't expect them to be big business builders. It would have been so much easier if someone had told me that up front.

I had a guy in my group named Ken. He seemed to be a 20 percenter, but he thought like an 80 percenter. He had been in the business for two years and built a residual income of about $500 per month. He came to me one night and said that the business wasn't really working for him. I asked him what he meant. He said, "I have been working hard for over two years and I'm only making $500 per month."

I said, "Ken, think about what you just said. You are making $500 per month, that's $6,000 per year, residually. You are not working to receive that money every month. Think about the asset you would need to have in the bank to generate $500 per month. Even if the bank gave you a 10 percent interest rate, you would have to have $60,000 cash in the bank. What could you have possibly done in the past two years to save $60,000?"

He said, "Nothing."

I said, "It's working pretty well, isn't it?"

He said, "I guess it is." Ken quit the business less than a year later.

I'll bet you are shaking your head right now, wondering, "What in the world was he thinking?" He did not have a good reason for leaving. He just wasn't patient enough. He wasn't able to see the job through because he was an 80 percenter. Case closed. Next! His decision was not my problem. I'm looking for the 20 percenters.

Another good friend is Rick. All he really wanted was to succeed in the business, but he had the "grass is always greener" disease. He is still in the profession today, but he has shifted gears, changed companies, switched downlines, and traded uplines. As a result, he has struggled to find the success he hoped for.

I believe the key to success in this industry is to be persistent. Failure cannot handle persistence. If you stay the course and do the simple things like list, share and sponsor, you will be successful. Every time you make a change, you basically start over. Rick understands that today, and I believe he has finally found a home in the industry.

Paul Orberson is a guy that I have always looked up to in this industry. Paul was the top income-earner in Excel and I loved to hear him speak. He made the business seem so easy. His approach was very direct. Either you were in or you were out. Paul's first goal was to make enough money to cover a new truck payment. Well, let's just say Paul got that new truck. Paul was the first person I ever knew who earned over one million dollars in one month.

One of Paul's goals was to give away $500 per day. If someone opened the door for him, he tipped them $20. When someone refilled his water glass at a restaurant, he tipped them $20. Paul is one of the most successful network marketers ever, and he still inspires me today. He is very humble. At our national conventions, he would be swarmed with people in the foyer of the hotel.

He once said, "The hand someone shakes now is the same hand that has taken out bank loans for houses and cars in the past. I'm able to do a few more things for my family and stuff, but I don't perceive myself as (being) any different than anybody else."

Paul told me one time that I would never be rich. I didn't understand what he was telling me then, but today I do. He told me it didn't matter how much money I made, I would never see myself as rich. When he told me that, I thought he was crazy but as we started to have some success in the business, I realized he was right. As our income increased, so did our expenses. The houses got bigger, the cars got nicer, and the planes got faster.

I have always lived my life at the edge of my means. That's not good! Even though we were making a lot of money each month, I never felt rich. I had a nice house. I drove a nice car. We went on great vacations each year, but I never felt like we had all the money we needed.

Paul was absolutely right. If you don't settle, if you continue to set goals and reach for more and try to help others, you will never be rich. I live my life with that philosophy today. I think that's why I have such a drive to keep working. A lot of people ask me why I work so hard. My answer is because I haven't reached all of my goals yet.

I first met **Al Thomas** at an Excel event in Dallas. It was our national convention, called Excelebration. He was amazing. He had it all. His enthusiasm and motivating speeches were something that I looked forward to.

Even with all the success he was experiencing, he always had time for me. He would sit down with Colleen and me and talk about our family, and he genuinely wanted to know how we were doing. That meant the world to us. When we were having a tough time getting our business going, Al was always willing to help. Today Al continues to build a multi-million-dollar organization and is one of the most successful network marketers in the world.

Jay and Meg Kelly-Smith are probably the most responsible for our success. They would call us each week just to check in. They lifted our spirits when we were down. They gave us ideas to improve our results. They looked at us as "their kids." We were so clueless. I think they felt sorry for us! They would come and speak at meetings for us. They would send us training material and brochures, and did everything they could to help us succeed. We were not even in their organization. The way I build my business today and the way I train others has their fingerprints all over it. The day we lost Jay Smith was a very sad day. His legacy lives through the hundreds of thousands of lives he has touched and that number grows every day.

Russ Noland became one my best resources and friends. He always had great advice and always made me laugh. Russ was the emcee at Excelebration and was very entertaining. Not only could he entertain the crowd, he knew how to build a business. Russ remains an icon in the network marketing industry. It was an honor to host events with a legend like Russ Noland.

None of these people were in my downline or my upline. They were just great people that became great friends who were willing to help. They remain my friends today.

The money you make from this industry is wonderful, but the friendships you develop will last a lifetime. You can't put a price tag on friendship. I'll talk more about that later.

Everyday Challenges

I continued to build my business in the best way I knew. I tried to soak up as much information as I could from others who were more successful than I was. With every new day came a different challenge. I had to report to school Monday through Friday by 8 a.m., and I could not leave that school building until 4 p.m. But at 4 p.m., it was my time! I gave teaching everything that I had. I took that responsibility very seriously, but when the teaching day was over, I devoted the rest of the day and night to building my dream.

I didn't coach. I didn't do any extracurricular activities. I did my job to the best of my ability. But if I was going to be the boss, I knew I had to go build my business and that's what I did.

excluding them. We looked at everyone who supported the local meetings as part of one team.

We were one team with one dream. Everyone pulled for one another's success. That's what made it work. We were like family. Many of those reps are our good friends today.

Each week our business presentations were an event. We had an overflow room for those who arrived late. We shut the door at 7:30 p.m. and started on time every time. Those in the overflow room had to watch the presentation on closed circuit television. Needless to say, most people arrived early to network and get the best seats.

It took us about three years to really get that kind of momentum going in Milwaukee. Now think about what I just said. Three years. Most people don't stick around for three weeks! I guess it comes down to how badly people really want to make a change in their lives.

I would meet people every day who needed the opportunity and were so excited to get started, but they would quit after the first person told them no. I never understood that. I once asked a guy, who quit about a week into his new business, why he ever signed up to begin with. I told him he should have just written the check to Steve Schulz instead of Excel. He just stared at me.

My friend **Loren Friedman**, who was a top income-earner, told me something very profound: "The people who tell you no won't make your house payment for you. They won't make your car payment. They won't educate your kids. They won't send the kind of money you want to your favorite church or charity and they won't send you on the kind of vacations you want to go on. So why would you listen to them? And the people who are telling you no and that this won't work, are probably broke! Don't take financial advice from people you don't want to be like financially." I loved his advice! I tell every rep I bring into the business the same thing. I want to prepare them for what is inevitably going to happen.

People will try to steal your dream because they don't have one of their own. I saw this happen almost every day. In this business you need to develop thick skin. Today, I dare people to tell me this profession won't work. In fact, it's kind of fun when they do, because I just shoot them out of the water.

Most people say no to the opportunity because they don't understand how it works. I try to educate them during the business presentation. I say things like, "Have you ever read a good book, seen a good movie, or had a meal at a good restaurant, and told someone about it?" The response is always "yes."

Then I say, "That's what we do too, but we get paid to refer people to our products and services. Let me show you what I mean." Then I go into the business presentation.

Please understand, it took me a while to develop that mindset. In the beginning, I took every "no" personally. I thought they were rejecting *me*. I had to learn how to handle rejection. I had to develop a "so what" attitude, and learn not to take it personally. People are not rejecting you. In most cases they are rejecting change. Also, some people are resistant to seeing you do something that doesn't fit their ideal of who you should be.

Think about it. Do your parents see you doing this business? My grandmother freaked out when I told her I was in this business. She saw me as a schoolteacher not an entrepreneur. She used to tell me to get a "good job." I look at that as an oxymoron today.

I'm telling you all this to shorten your learning curve. Everything I learned in this industry was "trial by fire." It was my goals that kept me from quitting. I had a very big reason to build this business, and I was willing to do whatever it took to reach my goals. That doesn't mean it wasn't difficult. I wanted to quit the business a thousand times. It's not easy when people tell you that you're nuts, you're crazy and that it will never work. It's not easy reaching your goals when people say, "You can count on me," and then they don't keep their word.

But my goals, Pat Hintze, and the hundreds of people I met at the events throughout the country kept me in the game. I could never let Pat down and I knew the people who were successful had nothing on me — except time. They simply had more time to collect more no's than I did. I feel the person who collects the most no's wins! I just needed more time.

I remember driving to Eau Claire, Wisconsin, on a Thursday night to do a business presentation. I left my school building at 4 p.m. and got to Eau Claire right at 7:15 p.m. I walked into the hotel and found the meeting room, hoping it would be packed with anxious people waiting to hear about my fantastic opportunity. When I got to the meeting room, it was empty. Not one person was there and the meeting was going to start in 10 minutes. I got the flip chart all set up. The nametags were on the registration table and I waited. At 8 p.m., I decided to pack up my flip chart and put away my name tags and drive back to Milwaukee. Not one person showed up — not even the rep who asked me to come do the meeting.

I drove all the way back to Milwaukee and pulled into my subdivision. My house light was the only light on and I thought to myself, "Either you are a complete idiot or you are a genius." I found out later that it was the latter! You see, when everyone is going one way, and you have the guts to go the other way, you can make millions! I reported to work the next day at 8 a.m. and waited for my next adventure. SW-SW-SW-SW: Some Will. Some Won't. So What. Some Waiting.

I knew I didn't need a lot of people to make a lot of money. I just needed a few good people. The few good people were the issue! I created and recreated my prospect list daily. I just started picking people off one at a time and getting them in front of the opportunity. I would do this over, and over, and over again in search of those few good reps.

There was a lady named June who was super excited about the business. She was on my fourth or fifth level. She asked me to meet with her husband and explain the opportunity because he was not very supportive of her decision to join. I went over to June's home on a Saturday afternoon after our training class, and her husband Ron met me at the door. He invited me in and we sat down at his kitchen table. I'm not sure why he was trying to intimidate me, but he was not very friendly.

I thanked him for meeting with me and I started the presentation. I got 30 seconds into it and he stopped me. He looked me in the eye with his arms crossed and said, "I just want you to know that I have absolutely no interest in you or your pyramid scam." I said, "That's fine, but I told your wife that I would explain the opportunity, and if you don't mind, I would like to continue." June had signed up as a managing representative. She didn't sign up as a trainer.

When I finished explaining the opportunity to Ron, he looked at me and said, "Well, it looks like we need to be trainers as well." Not only did Ron make a 180-degree turn about the opportunity, he was using the pronoun "we" when referring to himself and June working the business. He decided they needed to upgrade to the area coordinator training position.

That turned out to be a great meeting. That's a perfect example of why you need to get the information in front of people. Today, when I show someone the business, I don't worry if they sign up or not. I understand it's a numbers game. I just need to get the information in front of as many people as I can. As it turned out, Ron and June were part of our core group and they built a large organization.

Leap of Faith

About three years into building the business, our son Mike was born. Colleen and I were now outnumbered three kids, two adults. I was really excited when Mike was born. He was a great addition to our family. Mike also gave me another good reason to keep building my business. So then we had three children, ages zero, two and four. Our family was set. It was decision time.

Pat and I decided it was time for me to go full-time with the business. I was only making $23,000 a year as a teacher. My take home pay was $749 every two weeks. It didn't take much to replace that income. We figured the business would grow faster if I worked it full-time.

Pat was making over $80,000 a year with his paper sales position. He was committed to supporting two families if he needed to. When I went full-time, we were making somewhere between $3,000 and $4,000 per month. That number was deceiving because we were spending almost that amount in business expenses per month. My safety net was Pat's income.

The previous year I had told my colleagues at school that I was not coming back in the fall because my business was starting to take off. Well, I was back in the classroom that fall. All I heard that year was, "How's your little pyramid business going? Have you made your first million yet? Are you driving a pink Cadillac yet?"

It was tough. I played their little game and laughed on the outside, but inside, my blood was boiling. What they didn't realize was that their comments were actually helping me build my business. They were throwing gas on a fire that was already raging. I was more determined than ever to make this business work and fire my boss!

There were 62 teachers in my building and all of them knew I was working my Excel business. None of them would be a rep in my group, and only one would be my customer. She team-taught with me; she really didn't have a choice. None of the other teachers, principals, office workers, or custodians would help me out. I pretended I didn't care, but deep down inside, it killed me. But it didn't stop me.

Every morning I would go into the office and ask Shirley, our school secretary, the person who really ran the school, which teachers were out of the building for the day and I would get the names of the substitutes in their rooms. I would walk into each room and introduce myself and say, "I'm Steve. I'm over in fifth grade. If you need something, come across the hall and get me. By the way, are you looking for a full-time position?"

Now, if you are a teacher, you already know what the response was. Every substitute teacher said the same thing.

They said, "Yes! I thought if I started subbing in the district, I would get my foot in the door for a full-time job."

I said, "Great! I think there is going to be an opening right here in this building."

They said, "Whose?" I said, "Mine!"

They all replied, "Why, what are you doing?" I said, "I started my own business and I don't think I'm going to be working here much longer. Have you ever thought about starting your own business?"

Some said yes. Some said no. And some said maybe.

I said, "Great! I don't have time right now, but when do your kids go to music? When do your kids go to gym? What are you doing for lunch today? Do you have to leave at 4 p.m. or can you stick around for an extra 20 minutes?"

By using this approach, I sponsored four substitute teachers into my business and I sponsored the D.A.R.E. officer who came into my classroom to teach my kids. Those five people came to me. I didn't go to them. I just asked the right questions.

That year, my third year of teaching, I once again told my colleagues that this was it. This was definitely going to be my last year of teaching. I was putting a lot of pressure on myself, but I was determined.

At the end of the school year I said goodbye to my fellow teachers and told them I was not returning in the fall. Granted, I had not made it official with the administration quite yet. I had all summer to make it official.

As August approached, Pat and I decided it was time to make the move. I was not going back to the classroom. This was it. This was going to be a major turning point in my life.

I wanted it to happen and I thought I was ready to make the move, but I gave myself a way out.

I contacted the superintendent of schools and asked for a one-year leave of absence. I didn't tell any of my colleagues this. I was granted the leave of absence and I did not return in the fall. I knew if things didn't work out the following year, I could always go back to teaching.

When I did not report to my classroom in the fall of 1994, I waited by the phone to field calls from my fellow teachers. I knew they were going to want to know if I was OK, if anything was wrong, if there was anything they could do to help. I thought they might even call to congratulate me and wish me luck. I waited, and waited, and waited. No calls came in. Not one! Not one of my "friends" from my building was concerned for my well-being. I could not believe it. These people didn't care one bit. They had no interest in what I was up to or even if I was alive.

I lost a little bit of my faith in humanity during that time, but once again, it fueled my fire. I was out to prove all of them wrong. I didn't care if they wanted to be dead-broke teachers for the rest of their lives. All day long they would complain about the kids and about the money they made and I showed them a way out. None of them took it! So what! I didn't need them and I was about to prove it.

Being able to devote all of my time to my business, and not having to worry about not having a job if it didn't work out, was the magic formula. At first I was concerned that I would not have enough to do to keep me busy all day and all night. That concern faded quickly.

I ran ads. I sent out flyers. I pounded the streets and was willing to talk to anyone willing to talk to me. I felt I needed to build the business fast and relieve the pressure from Pat so he would not have to support two families. (We decided I would take any income from the business matching my teaching income. If the income was short of that amount, Pat would make up the difference out of his pocket. I did not want him to have to do that.) We both worked extremely hard and our checks started to grow. The plan was working. I worked full-time while Pat worked part-time, and it proved to be a winning combination.

Our approach was so simple that I often I wondered if we were missing something. All we tried to do was introduce people to the opportunity and ask them to join. It seemed like other reps were making it so complicated. They were sending out mass mailings. They were inviting prospects to these executive lunch meetings. They were holding nationwide conference calls and advertising on the radio and television. We couldn't afford to do any of that, so ours was a guerrilla marketing approach.

We taught our reps to make a list of the people they knew and invite them to come and look at the opportunity. We were not signing up thousands or even hundreds of people per month but we were growing. We would have 20 or 30 new reps join, and by teaching them to do the same thing we were doing, the system was working.

To this day, I teach the same things. I have reps that have been with me for over 23 years, and they always laugh because my training classes haven't changed. These reps laugh at my same stupid jokes and often finish my sentences for me. They do it because this has been working for all of us for over 20 years!

I don't want to change what's working. There is no need to fix what is not broken. I have seen so many people over the years who get bored and start making changes. They feel like they have to entertain the reps in the room. They feel the core group of reps will get tired of hearing the same old thing each week at training or at business presentations.

I've never felt that way. I guess I never thought the meetings were for the "old reps" anyway. I always thought meetings were for the new reps and guests. I once told my group that if they ever got bored at a business presentation or a training class it was their fault. You will NEVER be bored if you have guests or new reps with guests in the room.

If you walk into a business presentation or training and look around the room and see that 30, 40, or 50 percent of the people there are in your group, you will not be bored. You will be ecstatic. If you continue to do the same thing over, and over, and over, you will master it. If what you are trying to master is working, why would you ever change your approach?

After just a few months, I knew my teaching days were over. The business was growing and there was really nothing we could do to stop it. We had sponsored some really good people who were better than we were at the business. We edified them and gave them the spotlight as often as we could.

Roger Salick was one of those guys. He was a karate instructor who led an extraordinary life. He was a daredevil. I'm not kidding. He did some crazy things like jumping off moving trains or riding a bull in at the Calgary Stampede, things that few people have the guts to attempt. Roger was in a number of movies and was simply fascinating to talk to. He joined the business the same night he saw the opportunity. He looked at Pat and me and said, "We are going to make millions, boys!"

At his first business presentation he invited a lot of people. There must have been 40 or 50 people there because he asked them to attend. The best part was, when he invited someone to a business presentation, he always told them to bring someone as well. At that first meeting, his organization grew seven levels deep. He invited people who invited others who did the same. It was crazy! I was so excited for Roger — I didn't sleep much that night.

Pat and I had finally found someone who was as excited as we were and who understood how this business worked. We learned a lot from Roger. He was just one of those guys you loved to be around. He was full of energy and loved people. And people joined his group without even seeing a presentation. If Roger was in, they were in!

Making the decision to go full-time was a turning point in my life. It's easy to look back and see those times when you could have either turned left or right and your entire life would have been different. I am eternally grateful to Pat for having the confidence in me to make that move. It was a decision that changed both of our lives forever.

As our business grew, so did the accolades. People started recognizing us as pretty good business builders. We were mentioned in the company newsletters. We were featured in Excel's video program, "Profiles of Excellence." We weren't making huge money, but we were getting attention.

I still had my fellow teachers as a motivating factor. I know that sounds stupid, but it worked for me. It's too bad so few teachers get involved in this profession, because it's really perfect for them. The teachers who do get involved in this profession seem to be very successful.

As a teacher, I remember sitting in the teachers' lounge and listening to the negative chatter. I couldn't believe what I was hearing. The teachers complained about the kids. They complained about the parents. They complained about the administration and school policy. I thought these people would be perfect for my business. I was going to show them a way out of the mess they had gotten themselves into.

But when I approached them about the business, they had all the answers. They had no idea what the opportunity was about, but they knew it wasn't going to work. They would tell me to quit, not to get anyone else involved, that it was a pyramid scheme. I told them we all worked in a pyramid scheme. You would have thought I had just told them their baby was ugly!

These people were smart. They all had college degrees, but they were closed-minded when it came to my business. I had the solution for everything they were complaining about. I wasn't asking them to quit their jobs. I was asking them to build a business on the side. Think about building a business where your part-time income starts to exceed your full-time income. That sounds like a good problem to have.

None of them got it! Here's what I did. Every time I was mentioned in an article or written up in a book or I received an award, I would send a copy to the teachers' lounge. Yeah, it might sound juvenile, but so what? I wanted to prove just how wrong they were about me — and this opportunity. They were stuck in that classroom not making enough money while I was the boss, calling the shots, building a future that I had no chance of building as a teacher. Who's the smart one now?

It felt so good sending those articles to the school. I sat back and waited for the calls to start rolling in. They were going to be so proud of me. I made it! They were going to come begging to have me sign them up. It was going to be amazing. I even had the sign-up forms ready to go.

I waited, and waited, and waited. I decided the mail was slow and it was just a matter of time. I double-checked to make sure I sent my contact information with the articles. Everything was in place; the only thing that was wrong was nobody called me.

Can you believe that? I had the answers to their prayers and I was proving to them that it worked. Why didn't anyone call? Because they were not open to the opportunity, and thought they knew everything.

To this day I still send articles, books, videos, and award announcements to the teachers' lounge; I still haven't received one phone call. No one called to say, "Congratulations, Steve! Great job buddy, we knew you could do it!" I'm not sure any of the teachers I worked with are still there, but I don't care. It's therapy for me.

Here is the lesson in all of this: **Don't expect the other prisoners to be excited when you break out!** Do I need any of those teachers as my customers today? No. Do I need any of those teachers as a rep in my business today? No. Would I like to have them as either reps or customers today? Yes. But that's not the case, so I moved on. SW-SW-SW-SW: Some Will. Some Won't. So What. Some Waiting. Next!

I Have No Explanation

This really is a crazy business. There is no way of predicting who will be successful and who won't be. I've signed up people who I thought would be amazing and they didn't do anything. I've signed up people who I know spent their last $400 to get started and they turned out to be superstars.

Russ Noland once told me, "You can't tell the studs from the duds." That statement is so true. That's why it's important to learn to sort people out. I have no idea who will be successful and it's not my job to figure it out. My job is to show the business over, and over, and over. People actually sort themselves out.

The all-pro defensive end and Hall of Famer Reggie White was part of our organization in Wisconsin. Yes, that

Reggie White. I was so excited to be able to work with him; after all, who would say no to Reggie White?

No one would have if he had asked them. That was the problem. We couldn't get Reggie to do anything with the business. All he needed to do was tell people he was part of the program and they should be as well. But that never happened. I wonder if he just wanted to be a spokesman for Excel and get paid because he was Reggie White! He had no idea what he had in his hands.

Now you may be saying, "Come on Steve, Reggie doesn't need the money. He is a professional athlete."

Well, we have people in this profession who make a lot more than professional athletes. The average career of an NFL player is three and a half years. If professional athletes understood that, they would be looking for ways to supplement their playing income. A guy like Reggie White could have been the highest paid rep in this entire industry if he had truly understood the opportunity he had.

You can see the ups and downs I have faced in this business. I thought having a guy like Reggie White in the program would give us so much credibility that everyone would join. I was so disappointed. About two weeks after Reggie joined, he signed a contract to promote another phone company. I'm still shaking my head today.

On another occasion, I signed up a guy named Jack. He was a true networker; he tried everything. If it was multi-level, he was in. I didn't know that at the time, however. Jack worked very hard at his day job. He was married and had one son. He struggled every month financially. He was looking for the right opportunity to relieve some of his monthly financial pressure.

Jack answered an ad that I ran in the local newspaper. When I met with him, I felt I had known him my entire life. Jack was a great guy. He made no excuses. He said he didn't have the money to get started, but he assured me he would come up with it.

I never felt bad about working with people who didn't have the money to get started because I was offering them an opportunity to make money. And I knew that they would if they were coachable and followed the simple system that Pat and I had put together.

Jack was very coachable. He did exactly what he needed to do. He got people in front of the opportunity. It was just a matter of time before he found a player, a 20 percenter. Ted owned a computer repair store, and understood the importance of being the boss. Ted took off with the business. At that time, he was our strongest leader. He was awesome! Ted was able to conduct training classes with us and do weekly business presentations. He was a duplicate of Pat and me. It was perfect! Ted was promoted through the ranks very quickly. Jack was on cloud nine. I kept telling Jack, "Go find another Ted." He tried to do just that.

Well, a funny thing happened on the way to financial freedom. Ted suddenly forgot where he came from. He decided that he didn't need the team that helped him become the successful networker that he was. He started doing things HIS way, and came up with his own untried techniques. As a result, Pat and I decided not to let Ted participate in the local business presentations and trainings as a presenter; he wasn't following our proven system. Ted thought he would be better off on his own, so he opened his own training center on the other side of town and held meetings and trainings on the same days we held ours.

I can't think of any explanation for what Ted did. Why in the world would he completely abandon something that was working so well? Was Ted's ego really that big? It made no sense to me. We were giving him the stage, edifying him, and feeding his ego. I guess he wanted the building techniques to be based on his own ideas. Sometimes people just can't get out of their own way.

A few people followed Ted over to his new training center. He continued to build his group, and the people who joined couldn't tell the difference — at first.

In the meantime, Pat and I refused to give up on what was working for us. Word soon spread of the success we were having at our training center on Tuesday nights. We filled the room to capacity and then some every Tuesday and Saturday, and Ted's reps soon wanted to be a part of what we had. They slowly came over to our meetings and Ted started to struggle. He was not building as fast as he previously did. His techniques were not working and his ego was getting in the way.

When people asked Pat and I why Ted was now struggling so much, we would say, "Ted and his team are always welcome to join us, but if you can't keep up, take notes!"

We were not going to beg anybody to support our group. Our success was speaking for itself. Our attitude was, "You are always welcome, but don't wait for the formal invitation."

Here is another head-scratcher: Remember my sister Robin who would not join as a rep or even try the service and become my customer? To this day, after 23-plus years and all of the success we have had, she still isn't involved in my business. Think about that. If your brother made millions of dollars in a business you could start for about $400, wouldn't you be first in line to find out how you could do the same?

My sister Robin was in a little financial trouble. She had some business debt and some credit card debt she needed to take care of. She initially wanted to consolidate all of her debt into one payment. Not bad thinking — many people would do the same.

Here's where the story will blow your mind. Robin eventually called me and asked me to give her a substantial amount of money to pay off this debt and help her get into a new building for her business. I patiently listened to her proposal, which wouldn't have benefited me at all; she wasn't going to pay me any interest and I was supposed to assume all of the risk. Apparently, she thought my last name was Visa or American Express or U.S. Bank. As I listened, I thought to myself, "Are you kidding me? If you would have joined my business, you would not be in this situation today, asking me for money." You see, I had no problem with Robin not signing up as a rep, but I had a huge problem with her not signing up as a customer. I wasn't asking her for a kidney — I was asking her to be my customer and save some money.

She was now asking me for a ton of money to help her out, when she was not willing to try my service and help me out. I gave her a lot of credit for asking. Her risk on this deal was zero, while mine was a small fortune. I think at one point I even laughed out loud.

Please tell me, as you read this, that you are in my corner. Do you understand what was going through my head as she explained this deal to me? Don't I have a right to be a little bitter? Don't I have the right to completely tell her off? Don't I have the right to tell her how completely unfair this deal is? I am totally in the driver's seat here.

So guess what I did? Yep, I gave her the money. Just because *she* doesn't get it doesn't mean that *I* don't get it. She is my sister. She needed my help. Of course I was going to help her. It's not my fault that she didn't feel the same way.

I'm going to tell you something and you can choose to believe it or not: I truly believe we all have people in our lives, who are very close to us, who don't necessarily want us to succeed. How else can I explain why my sister wouldn't even try my phone service?

Let me explain it this way: If you take a bucket of crabs and place that bucket near water, eventually one of the crabs will start scaling the side of the bucket in an effort to try and get out. But just before the crab can reach up and pull himself out, another crab will reach up and pull him back down.

I like to consider myself one of the crabs that got out of the bucket, and I'm looking down at all my friends and family members saying, "Get out of the bucket! I did! I will help you. My hand is halfway down — just grab onto it."

But some people think it's easier to reach up and try to pull you back down to their level than it is for them to work real hard to come up to yours. I can't think of any other way to explain it.

Here is what I believe is fundamentally wrong with the multilevel marketing profession: We ask you to go out and talk to the people you know. The problem is, those people know you. *That* is the issue.

When you talk to your friends and family members about your business, what are you promoting? You are promoting extra income and flexible time. That's what this profession offers everyone. I don't care which company it is; the bottom line comes down to big money and free time. Everyone would love to make more money and have the time to enjoy it, but very few people are willing to do what it takes to get there.

Your friends and family members know you too well. They will look at you and say, "What do you know about making money? I can see the car you drive. I know where you live."

In most cases, YOU and BIG MONEY don't go together. It didn't for me. I was a dead-broke schoolteacher trying to tell people how to make money. It was very difficult to do, especially with the people who knew me best. Sometimes it's easier to talk to people you don't know since they don't have any preconceived notions about you. That is what happened to me. It might be different for you. You might have extremely supportive friends and family around you. But if you don't, be prepared to get a little beat up.

My brother Bill signed up with the business as soon as he turned 18. He was super excited and wanted to build a big business. At 18 years old, he lacked some credibility. He knew that, but he continued to build anyway. At one point, he was the youngest Executive Director in Excel. I even asked him to conduct training classes. Everyone loved him. He was young, good looking, a great speaker, and he was building a successful organization. I was proud of him. It was a nice feeling working with him.

In this business there are ups and downs if you're not careful. You can build your organization to 100 reps and have it fall back down to 10. It's just the way it works. It's a rollercoaster ride that most people are not prepared for. Bill's organization hit one of those lulls. He had more people quitting the business than joining. He did not understand the 80/20 rule. He became bitter with his reps, with Excel, and with me. He started blaming me for all of his problems. Somehow, everything that went wrong was my fault.

He didn't understand the numbers. He didn't understand that you can't change the 80/20 rule. Once again, I wasn't going to let him or anyone steal my dream. I was not going to drag anyone across the finish line of success. I tried to explain to him that it wasn't anybody's fault. I told him he just didn't have the right people yet and to keep talking and keep building.

If you take your eye off your target, it's pretty easy to miss it! That is exactly what Bill did, and what all of the 80 percenters do. They look for excuses to stop working, and they don't have to look too hard to find reasons to quit. They are all over the place. The difference between my brother Bill and the 20 percenters in this business is that the 20 percenters have really important goals. Those goals are so important that they won't let anything get in the way of accomplishing them.

I told Bill he could quit anytime he wanted to, but I also encouraged him to consider the alternatives. I asked him if he wanted to get a job working for someone else and spend the rest of his life building that person's dream. That's exactly what he did. He has since bounced from one job to another, and has never made the kind of money he used to dream about. Go figure. If he would have just stuck with me, I can guarantee things would have been different.

Early on, I realized this business is all about being persistent. As a result, I tried to do something with my business every day. I made a new contact, set up a business presentation or trained a new rep every day. I refused to lose. Failure cannot handle persistence.

My sister Angie, who is very supportive, is not in my business either. She lives in Arizona. I will never forget what she told me one day. She said, "If you lived out here, I could do this business." I told her that Jordan Adler lived about 15 miles from her. He would help her. She could go to his meetings. She still didn't join and is not in my business today.

This is what I've heard from my family members for years:

"You have the right personality."

"You could sell ice to an Eskimo."

"You got in at the right time."

"You're so good at talking to people."

"I could never do what you do."

This made me scream! They didn't have to be me. They could let ME be ME with their contacts.

I have no explanation as to how my siblings can see the success that I have had in this industry and still not want to be a part of it. If you want to be successful, find successful people and do what they do.

Major Turning Point

It's funny how my goals changed as the business grew. My first goal was to make enough money to make my car payment. My car payment was $203 per month. I remember Colleen saying to me, "If we could just get a free car out of this thing, that would be terrific." She called it "that phone thing."

We hit that goal pretty quickly. Then I thought we could make enough money to make our house payment. The idea of earning enough cash to pay for our house and car was intriguing. Colleen said, "Maybe we can make enough money so I can stay home with the girls." Sure enough, that happened. That's when I decided I wanted to stay home as well.

About a year and a half after I went full-time, we decided Pat needed to fire his boss as well. This was another major turning point in our business. Our safety net was now gone. It was sink or swim. Fear was a great motivator.

Pat and I both started working the business full-time. We really didn't do anything different; we just did more of the same. We had breakfast and lunch meetings along with home and hotel meetings. We knew if we were going to make the kind of money we saw others making, we needed to keep busy. At that time, all of us — Colleen and I and Pat and his wife, Cindy — began working the business full time.

Something that is still important to me today is the art of setting goals. I need to have a goal to run to. Every time I hit a goal, I set another one. I went from wanting to make enough money to cover my car and house payment to wanting to make enough to allow Colleen and me to stay home. In the back of my mind, my ultimate goal was to make $5,000 per month. I thought that if I could make $5,000 per month it would be nirvana! I used to make $23,000 per year and my goal would take me to $60,000. How could it get any better?

It got better, a lot better! I never stopped setting goals and we just kept hitting them. I realized that the day I stopped setting goals was the day I would start dying. When I had a goal to reach, I woke up with a purpose. Every day brought me closer to whatever my goal was. I've been doing that for more than 23 years now.

On one occasion, I was on my way to St. Louis to give a presentation. As I walked out the door, I felt a little tug on my jacket. I looked down and it was my seven–year-old daughter Emily. She looked up at me with her big blue eyes and said, "Can't those stupid people in St. Louis do it themselves?"

It's not that Emily had anything against the people in St. Louis; she did not even know them. It was a little girl's way of crying out, wondering why Dad had to go away. I explained to

Emily why I had to go, and then I looked at Colleen and told her we needed to involve the kids in our business.

From that point forward, we asked the kids to take part in our goal-setting process. Every New Year's Eve, we asked the kids what they wanted to get out of the business for the upcoming year. It was great. They had all kinds of ideas. They knew exactly what they wanted.

Megan and Emily wanted trips to Disney World and fun vacations on the beach, while Mike would often settle for a new bike or skateboard. This gave the kids ownership in the business. It became a lot easier for all of us when I had to leave on business trips because they knew they had a stake in the results. Sometimes one of the kids would still ask why I had to leave. I would walk them over to the refrigerator and remind them of the goal they had set and tell them that I had to go away and work once in awhile in order to achieve that goal.

This system worked perfectly. We experienced many great vacations and created lasting memories from goals the kids had set. They became my biggest cheerleaders. They were pulling for my success because that created success for them. It was a win-win situation.

I remember one vacation we took to Marco Island, Florida. We had a suite at the Marriott Hotel right on the beach. It was beautiful. The weather was perfect, the food was great and the entertainment was inspiring. We wanted to buy a condo on the island, so we called a realtor and had him show us a few properties.

The condo I fell in love with was on the top floor of a spectacular building. The unit was 6,200 square feet. It had everything, including a panoramic view of the Gulf of

Mexico. The price tag was $3.4 million, and we started trying to figure out a way to buy the property.

The next day we rented WaveRunners and went on a tour. We saw a lot of sea life, including dolphins, manatees and sea turtles. When we got back to the beach, Emily and I decided to take one more lap around the area. I stopped the WaveRunner in front of the condo we wanted to purchase.

Emily, who was 10 years old, said, "You know dad, if we buy that condo, this will be the only place we will ever go on our vacations. Don't you want to see other places on our vacations?"

She was absolutely right. My little 10-year-old girl was giving her dad million-dollar advice. She made it sound so simple. It was so clear to her. She made me realize the condo was a terrible deal for us and we did not make an offer.

My kids have been all over the world thanks to this business. They have been in places that I never had a chance of seeing on a teacher's salary. I took Megan on a trip to Europe. We played tourist in London and Manchester, England. We visited all of the major sites in just three days. Megan was only 13.

I took Megan and Emily on separate trips to Hawaii. That's where Emily and I learned to surf. Mike has been to Ghana, Thailand, and Australia. Megan spent an unforgettable two weeks in China. Emily has had memorable trips to Australia, New Zealand, South Africa, and Cambodia.

We've also taken family vacations to Mexico, the Dominican Republic, and the Bahamas. These experiences are priceless. We've made new friends all over the world.

One of my dream goals was to build a new home. Our house in West Allis was nice, but once again, I wanted more. We bought a lot in Oconomowoc, Wisconsin. The school system was good and the kids were excited to move. We had a friend from college, a designer for a local builder, help us with the blueprints. We were able to build the 3,000-square-foot home of our dreams (at least at that time). We loved that house. The kids all had their own rooms, and the finished basement made for a great game room. The neighborhood was full of kids the same age as ours. It was the perfect situation for raising our family.

There was a manmade ski hill at the end of our subdivision. The kids spent many Friday nights and Saturdays on that little hill. We gave them walkie-talkies so they could communicate with us. We could watch them ski from our house. Only in Oconomowoc would they have a manmade ski hill. It was part of a University of Wisconsin project back in the '60s. Oconomowoc is in the heart of the lake country, surround by flat land. The ski hill is certainly not natural to the environment and sticks out like a sore thumb, but it makes for great conversation.

A few years after we moved into our house, we decided to put in a pool. We thought it would be the perfect addition to our dream home. We picked out the shape. We designed the pool deck. We met with the landscapers and we picked out the fence. The entire project was only supposed to take three weeks. I thought that was amazing. Only three days passed between the time they dug the hole and the time they filled the pool with water! The landscaping, the lighting and the fence took longer to complete. The contractor who installed the pool fence was very knowledgeable. He was a perfectionist and his work was flawless. We had a number of brick pillars and each was topped with lights. The pool looked so good at night. It was the ideal home for entertaining, but it took awhile to get there.

As we were deciding where the fence and the brick pillars would be placed, we knew they were going to butt up against the property line of the lot next to us. The lot next to our home had been purchased by a builder who was going to build a spec home, but had not yet started the construction.

We eyeballed the property line and made our decision regarding the location of the fence. I knew we were close, but if we were over the line, I didn't think it could be any more than six inches or so. I was fine with our decision, but Colleen was a bit more nervous.

Construction started on the fence. The eight brick pillars were installed first, each at a cost of about about $1,200. As the pillar next to the property line was completed, Colleen decided to call in a surveyor to make sure we built the pool and fence on our lot.

That day I was playing golf. I was on the 16th tee getting ready to use my seven iron to hit a ball 150 yards during one of my best rounds of the year. Just before I hit my tee shot, my cell phone rang. It was Colleen. She said, "You need to come home, now! We're not six inches over the line, we are six feet over."

Calmly, I told her I would be right home. I explained to the guys I was playing with what had happened. My friend Wayne, a very successful salesman who gave me a lot of financial advice, walked up to the tee box, placed his ball on the tee and stuck his drive about four feet from the cup. He bent down, picked up his tee, looked at me and said, "Why don't you just buy the lot next door?" The idea was ingenious, except for the fact that the lot was already sold.

When I got home, I called the builder who owned the lot that I had just built my pool on. I asked him if the property was for sale and what was he asking for it. To my utter shock, he said the lot was for sale and he was asking $35,000. I almost fell off my chair, not because of the price, but because the lot was actually for sale. The builder told me he had decided not to build on the property and was selling it. I didn't tell him that I lived next door, or that my pool was encroaching on his land. I offered him $30,000 and he said, "No, I need to get $35,000 for it." I told him I would bring him a check that day. I'm sure he almost fell off of his chair.

That proved to be one of the best investments we ever made. The extra lot made a perfect backyard. I landscaped it with just grass, no trees or shrubs. I wanted to keep it wide open for games and for possible resale someday. The kids played countless soccer, softball, and kickball games on that lot. The dogs would chase the tennis ball for hours on that lot. We loved having the extra space.

The lot and house served its purpose for the next seven years. We made some very close friends in that neighborhood and so did the kids. We ended up selling the house and the extra lot separately. We sold the lot for $93,000. Not a bad six-year investment.

By then, Pat and I were playing a bigger role on the corporate side of Excel. Our faces were all over the business' presentation and training videos. We were also corporate trainers. We traveled worldwide conducting high-level training classes — we taught the teachers. Small training classes included 150 people, while some drew more than 2,000.

I did a training class in Germany and we needed to have a translator in the room — even with a last name like Schulz, my German was pretty rusty. Check that. It was nonexistent. Everyone in the room was wearing headphones. I would speak and then pause to let the translator do his thing, and then I would continue. That was the most difficult speaking engagement I ever did.

When speaking in public, timing is critical. When you are working with a translator, the timing is off. When I told a joke, I had to wait 30 seconds for the laugh that most of the time never came. The biggest problem was that the translator was funnier than I was! I got through the day and everyone had a good time, but I decided I needed to stick to English-speaking countries.

I did some training in England. On one occasion, I was preparing to leave the United States on a Wednesday. On the Sunday night before that, Megan came into my office and asked if she could come with me. I thought about it for roughly three seconds and then said yes. She was in seventh grade and I thought she could miss a few days of school. She would learn more on this trip than she could in school for those three days.

We arrived at London's Heathrow Airport. It was the craziest airport I have ever been to, and I fly a lot! One of my English reps picked us up and drove us to our hotel in a little town about 45 minutes outside of London. Getting used to driving on the opposite side of the road was the first learning experience for Megan and me.

When we finally got to our hotel room, Megan burst into tears. The room was about the size of an airplane bathroom. It was the smallest hotel room I had ever seen. We decided to jump on a train and head back to London in search of another place to stay. Remember, this was our first trip to Europe and we had no clue where we were going.

We packed a small bag and boarded the train that took us to King's Cross. When we got off the train, we found ourselves in a sea of people all rushing around with a purpose.

Megan and I had no purpose. We just started walking down the streets of London. I booked a room at the first hotel we saw. They could have charged me 1,000 pounds per night and I would have paid it. We just needed a room for a couple of nights. The room was beautiful.

We decided to do a little sightseeing, which turned into a lot of sightseeing. We rode the London Eye, toured the Tower of London, saw the royal family's jewels, visited Westminster Abbey, Big Ben, London Bridge (it's not falling down by the way), Piccadilly Circus, and Buckingham Palace — all in a day and a half.

The only thing we didn't find in London was good food. Luckily, there was a Pizza Hut; we ate there for breakfast, lunch and dinner! That was an amazing trip. What made it so special was having Megan there with me. We still talk about that trip today.

Each year at the international Excelebration conference, Pat and I would move up on the top earners' list. We went from number 43 to 26 then 23. It was a challenge each year just to make it into the top 50. The year we finished 23rd, I told Pat we have 23 good reasons to wake up each morning. My goal was to be number one. I knew that was a stretch because the top income-earner was making over a million dollars a month. Yes, seven figures a month!

Between 1994 and 1998 things were crazy with the business. Excel became the fastest growing company and hit a billion dollars in sales. Some cities had weekly business presentations of 700-plus people. Thousands of people were joining every day.

Kenny Troutt, the founder of Excel, would take some of the top income-earners on tours around the country. We came up with clever names for the tours: Executive Wave

Tour, Excel Night Out Tour, and the Presidential Wave Tour. Thousands of people would attend these events. We were treated like rock stars. People would stand in line and wait for autographs. Others wanted to shake our hands and say hello. Some had tears in their eyes and thanked us for changing their lives. It was an amazing feeling. The money we were making was great, but the people we were helping made it even more worthwhile.

We participated in an event in Indianapolis, Indiana, one January. Kenny Troutt was the featured speaker and I was doing the business presentation. Kenny flew in on his private jet and I met him at the hotel. The weather was not doing us any favors as four to eight inches of snow was predicted. But that did not stop the reps from turning out. We had about 1,800 people in attendance that night.

Kenny and I both needed to be in Dallas the next morning so we planned to fly out together that night. Kenny told me to hurry through the business presentation, and he cut his speech short to increase our odds of beating the storm.

After Kenny finished speaking, we headed out the back door of the auditorium. There was a limousine waiting to take us to the airport where Kenny's Gulfstream V was waiting for us. The two pilots were already on the plane when a young lady got on. I looked at Kenny and said, "Who's that?"

He said, "Our flight attendant."

I thought to myself, "What? We can't get our own drinks?" Kenny just looked at me and started laughing. He gave me a high five and said, "Good job tonight."

They plowed a path to the runway and then we were off to Dallas. That night changed my life. That was the first time I had flown in a private jet. My vision grew tenfold. I realized I had to expand my goals and thinking. There was still so much I needed to achieve. I had never thought about owning my own jet until that night in Indy.

One of my favorite quotes is from Les Brown: "Shoot for the moon. Even if you miss, you'll land among the stars." What that means to me is, dream big! Start thinking differently. People who make millions of dollars have a different thought process.

I was hanging around people who saw life in a totally different way than I did. They would talk in thousands when I was talking in hundreds. They were talking about the houses they were going to build, which included full-time security guards. They talked about the color of the planes they were looking to buy. The jewelry they were wearing took my breath away. Since I was part of the group, I needed to start thinking like they did. That night in Indiana took my thinking to the next level, which took my business to new heights.

On the next few pages, I share some of my photos with you — the results of dreaming big!

Above: View from our home in Lac LaBelle, Wisconsin. Below: On our way home from Mexico.

Above: Steve talks strategy with business partner Pat Hintze. Below: Colleen Schulz, Steve Smith, Steve Schulz, and Kenny Troutt.

Above: Steve Schulz receives the Jay Smith Excellence in Training Award, presented by Meg Kelly-Smith, center, and Jordan Adler. Below: Christmas 2013.

Above: Emily at an orphanage in Mozambique. Below: Fun on the water.

Above: Emily bungee jumping in New Zealand. Below: Emily, Colleen and Megan in Mexico.

Above: Steve, Colleen & Emily in Las Vegas. Below: Mike, Colleen and Megan after the Rock-n-Sole half marathon.

Above: Emily, Mike & Megan in Playa Del Carmen Mexico. Below: Mike in Ghana.

Above left: Family trip to Lambeau Field. Right: Mike & Emily at our home in West Allis, Wisconsin. Below: Mike in the whitewater of Fiji.

Above: Megan at the Great Wall in China. Below: Emily's new best friend.

Above: Emily in Australia. Below: Emily rappelling in Swaziland.

Our dream home in Oconomowoc, Wisconsin.

Above: Emily teaching nursing skills in Cambodia. Below: Steve on Lac LaBelle.

Game On

Every morning I would wake up and hit the ground running. I was motivated to continue building the business. There was so much more I wanted to accomplish. As I became better friends with people like **Randy and Melissa Davis, Chuck and Sandra Hoover, Phillip and Heidi Eckhart, John and Patrice Jones, Ronny Kirkland, Mike and Barbara Lammons, Kevin Pine, Jimmy and Kathy Dick, Beth Henson, Lee and Rhonda Lemons, Bob and Phil Mims, Scott and Janet Pospichal**, and many more, I couldn't believe how small I used to think. How limited my dreams were!

Those people were amazing. They were all building multimillion-dollar organizations and living the lifestyle to prove it. Their homes were right out of "Lifestyles of the

Rich and Famous." Their cars were more luxurious than my house. The jewelry they were wearing looked like it had just come off the red carpet in Hollywood. They had a vision I didn't even know existed.

Pat and I decided to set bigger goals, and we knew if we were going to reach those goals, we needed to work even harder. We came up with a crazy idea to get a booth at as many trade shows as we could. The goal was to sign up thousands of customers who would use the phone service.

Excel was running a promotion, giving people a chance to receive two free round-trip airline tickets to Hawaii, Cancun, Jamaica, Orlando, Puerto Vallarta, or New Orleans, just for trying the phone service. The new customers had to stay one week at a participating hotel, but there were four to six hotels to choose from at each location. It was a great deal.

We included various leaders from our group to help staff the booth, and we divided up the customers. We set up a booth at the home show, the car show, the boat show, and the mall — basically anywhere we could find people.

We were customer-gathering machines. There were four to five people working the booth from 10 a.m. to 10 p.m. Depending on the venue, we would sign up over 100 new customers per day. During one summer, we signed up over 6,000 customers just by working the booth on the weekends. It was crazy! People wanted the airline tickets. They didn't really care about the money they would be saving on their phone bills.

We were so proud of ourselves. We thought this was the best way to generate residual income. We talked to Kenny Troutt about our success and he really didn't say much. He didn't congratulate us. He didn't even want us to tell other people what we were doing. I could not figure out why he wasn't as excited as we were.

Reality set in about three months later. We noticed a lot of personal customers and customers in our downline were canceling the service. In less than a year, 95 percent of those 6,000 customers had cancelled.

Executive Vice President of Marketing Steve Smith called Pat and me to talk about how we were building the business. He told us that we were completely wrong in our thinking, that this business is built on relationships. It's not about a few people doing a lot — it's about a whole bunch of people doing a little. He also said it's not about gathering hundreds of customers; it's about getting a few reps to gather a few customers who then repeat the process. He saw what was happening to our customers and he understood why. The reason our customers were leaving almost as fast as we were signing them up was because we had no relationship with them.

The customers who signed up with us at the mall, the home show or the boat show, were the same people who signed up with AT&T or MCI the following week when they were offered another incentive. It wasn't about the phone service to these people; it was about the free beach towel Sprint was giving away. These people would sign up with any company that had an incentive. I was sick. I wanted to cry. After all was said and done, the only customers we had remaining were the original 23 we signed up during the first two weeks. Those customers were loyal. Those people would never switch back because of the relationship we had with them.

I was starting to figure out this profession. It took a hit over the head with a two-by-four, but I was starting to see the light. It was no wonder Steve and Kenny did not want us to teach others what we were doing when I suggested that we do a workshop at the national convention on customer gathering. They did not even return my call. It turned out we were the worst customer gatherers in the company!

We decided it was a lesson learned. We needed to get back to the basics and start gathering reps and teaching them to gather a few customers. What we were doing was not duplicable. Did I really think the people in my group were all going to set up booths at shows all over the country? Even as I tell you this story, I'm shaking my head.

After the conversation with Steve Smith, I decided to simplify my business. I did not worry about customers and concentrated on getting new reps into the business. I finally realized that companies need customers to survive, which is why they build a customer requirement into the compensation plan for all of the reps. If you don't gather a certain number of customers, you don't get paid. Pretty simple, right? Think of it this way: If you want to get paid for having 1,000 loyal customers in your group, it is a lot easier to find five reps, who find five reps, who find five reps, and then allow all of those reps to gather just 10 loyal customers.

So the effort you put in is finding five reps and gathering 10 personal loyal customers, but you get paid for over 1,000 loyal customers! Isn't that nuts? Sometimes I bang my head against the wall wondering why everyone doesn't get started in this profession.

After we changed our approach and concentrated on building reps, everything changed. We started to see major jumps in our monthly commission checks. I was actually bringing home more money than I needed to live on, and was able to start saving some money. What a concept!

We sometimes saw monthly increases in our income between $4,000 and $8,000. We thought we had made it!

But then the next month, the check would drop by $3,000. I could never figure out the pattern. The only thing I knew was that I needed to keep talking to people and showing them the business. I did not need to think about anything else. I always tried to lead by example. If the people in my group saw me bringing guests to the business presentations and signing up new people monthly, I hoped they would do the same. It worked! The 20 percenters were moving the group.

Our check hit $40,000 in one month. The next month it was more than $80,000. We couldn't believe it! We thought there had to be a mistake, but we didn't wait around to find out. We cashed the check immediately.

I thought our check would easily be more than $100,000 the next month, but it was only for $57,000. We thought the world was coming to an end. I couldn't believe it. I wondered what had happened to the $100,000 it was supposed to be. How soon I forgot where I came from. I was making $57,000 in one month compared to $1,500 when I was teaching. Not too bad. I was quickly reminded of the 80/20 rule. We had a lot of 80 percenters in the group. The goal was to build the core group of 20 percenters.

The income continued to rollercoaster up and down. I talked to other leaders and they told me that they were going through the same thing. I was starting to understand the dynamics of building a business like this — wait, THERE ARE NO DYNAMICS! I could not figure this business out at all.

Sometimes Pat and I would just laugh because there was no rhyme or reason as to why some things happened in the business. Like I said before, the people we thought would be great ended up doing nothing, and the ones we thought would struggle turned out to be our biggest players.

As Pat and I were building the business, we did not see each other very much. We were always heading in different directions. If we were in the same room, it was counterproductive. We could cover a lot more ground if we did separate meetings. The only time we were together was on Tuesday nights for our big meeting of the week in the Milwaukee area. After the meeting, we got together and talked strategy or laughed about what had happened the previous week.

One time, we found ourselves with some money to play with. When we asked Kenny Troutt about investments, he told us that we should never invest our money on our own. He said we would find out what terrible investors we really were if we tried. That was one piece of advice that we did not take from Kenny. We decided we knew more than Wall Street. We picked a few companies and invested in them using a day-trading strategy. The stock prices of the companies we chose started to rise quickly. We got smarter by the day!

We let the stock ride to a point where we were both up over $1 million. In our infinite wisdom, we were sure the stock was going to split and we were going to double our money. The stock price started dropping but we knew better. It was just some people taking profits and the price would start rising in a few days.

In a few days, the stock was sitting at half the value it had only one week prior. We believed so much in those companies and wanted to prove our abilities as investors, but we finally sold our stock. I put about $60,000 in my pocket and Pat made about $48,000, but we lost almost $1 million each in one week! Weren't we great? Weren't we wonderful? Pigs get fat, but hogs get slaughtered.

Kenny was right. The lesson here was *stay in your lane!* Surround yourself with experts. Don't try to do things you are not qualified to do. Swallow your pride and things will work out for the better.

As our friendship with the top income-earners grew, our vision stretched. Kenny Troutt and Steve Smith did a great job of putting the top income-earners in the spotlight. They wanted the rest of the company to see the lifestyle that the opportunity could provide. We were all chasing the dream of financial independence. It was all about the lifestyle. Sure, the phone service would help people by saving them a little money, but it was the commission we made by telling those few people about the savings that we were all after.

Think about it this way: If you had the cure for cancer, wouldn't you tell everyone? What if you got paid to tell everyone? That's how Excel was for us. I couldn't wait to wake up every morning and talk about the opportunity for others to become financially free. ***It was all about the money!*** I didn't talk about the service. I talked about freedom, the freedom to live the life people had always dreamed about — one they were never going to achieve while working at their current jobs.

I had the solution. It was up to each individual to take hold of what I had. I didn't care if they joined. I just ran the numbers. SW-SW-SW-SW: Some Will. Some Won't. So What. Some Waiting.

•

Steve Smith, a.k.a. Captain Fun, owned a massive ranch outside of San Antonio, Texas. He would often invite groups comprised of the top leaders to spend the weekend there. The place was amazing. Steve had zebras on his ranch. I'm not sure that was even legal, but it was so cool!

The ranch was a place where everyone really got to know one another. We all slept in one room and shared one bathroom. The bunks were all lined up together; we felt like the Waltons when the lights were turned out. Our cell phones didn't even work. This was all by design. We played tennis, went on hikes, swam in the pool, fished in the bass-stocked ponds, and ate really well. Steve had a full-time staff at the ranch and feeding his guests was something they loved to do. I'm sure we all gained 10 pounds when we were at the ranch.

At night, we sat around the campfire and shared stories. Everyone had a story or two to tell. **Chuck Hoover**, who became one of my best friends, told the best stories. His listeners were often on the ground, doubled over with laughter. Chuck was very animated in his storytelling and never spilled a drop of his beloved Crown and Coke. He brought that everywhere! Chuck and I were holding an event in Houston one night. Just before I was introduced to go on stage, Chuck came over to me and said, "Here, take a big drink of this Diet Coke before you go up there." I grabbed his glass and downed what I thought was Diet Coke. He had forgotten to tell me about the Crown Royal part of the drink. In fact, I'm not sure any Diet Coke had made it into the glass. Needless to say, I was ready! We lost Chuck a few years ago, but his memory will live with me forever.

Steve loved airplanes and helicopters, and he owned some of both. He gave us helicopter tours of the ranch. I could have flown around in that thing all day. I loved it and I wanted one! Pat and I talked about taking the helicopter to our weekly meetings in Chicago, Green Bay, or Madison. It was just a different way of thinking. It was outside the norm, but who wanted to be normal!

One day at the ranch, a few of us guys were at Steve's residence talking about the new helicopter he was thinking about buying. We talked about the color scheme. We talked about cloth verses leather and the size of the engine. It was just guy talk. Later that night as we were all sitting around the campfire, Colleen and I were on one side and Steve and his wife, Sarah, were on the opposite side. I very innocently asked Steve when he thought he was going to get his new helicopter. Steve's wife Sarah spun around, looked at him and said, "We're getting a new helicopter?" Now, you know you have made it when you can buy a new helicopter and not tell your spouse!

I sat there in utter amazement. Steve was shopping for planes and helicopters the way I shop for cars. I guess that's not really true because I would at least tell Colleen I was buying a new car. My head was spinning. I watched as the wives admired each other's diamonds and the guys compared watches that cost more than the down payment of my house.

Steve invited us to the ranch to network with the other leaders and to expand our vision. He succeeded! Every time I left the ranch I became more excited about my work. It seemed as though Steve Smith had a soft spot in his heart for Pat and I. Maybe he just felt sorry for us because we struggled for so long, but never quit. Steve would often come to Milwaukee and participate in our meetings. That was a big help. Our biggest crowds showed up when Steve Smith came to town.

I would start off with the business presentation, Pat would do his normal "can't miss" close, and then Steve would do his thing. He would get up in front of the room and make people feel like they could really succeed in this business. He would talk in that slow Texas drawl and have the audience in the palm of his hand. Everybody loved Steve, including the guests who had no clue who he was.

He made the business sound so easy. He made people feel sort of foolish if they didn't get started. Steve would talk for about 45 minutes and say the same thing over, and over, and over. He would say, "If you go get some customers and show a few other people how to gather a few customers, we'll pay you."

That was his entire business presentation. He made people assume the service was good. He helped reps realize that they did not have to teach anyone how to use the phone, or know how deep the cables were. That's why Excel was so successful. The success was in its simplicity. Everyone could do it. It was never, "Can you do it?" It was always, "Will you do it?"

Steve taught me posture. He told me to never beg anyone to join my team. He said, "Present the opportunity in a way that is understandable and ask them to join. Then do it again." Every rep across the country was giving the same business presentation. It was one of the smartest things Excel did. They created a cookie cutter system. It was the McDonald's theory: No matter what McDonald's restaurant you go to, the menu and layout of the building are the same.

Excel even had "goon squads" showing up at local business presentations to make sure the presenters were all compliant. This served two purposes. First, it kept Excel out of trouble with any regulatory agencies, and second, every rep knew what they needed to do. There was one PowerPoint presentation and one business presentation script. No one had to reinvent the wheel.

Since I was the presenter on the corporate business presentation video, I gave the presentation word-for-word according to the script, from 1996 to 2004. I loved it and hated it at the same time. Mostly, I hated the taping of it, since it had to be done in one take with no teleprompter! It often took hours to tape a 30-minute video.

The Main Event

There was no doubt that the national convention was the highlight of the year. Our calendar year ran from August to July. Excelebration was usually held in Dallas, each year in August, and the weather could be brutal. Often, it was more than 100 degrees with very high humidity. Still, thousands of people attended Excelebration. But it wasn't always like that.

The first national convention I attended was in 1991. There were only about 300 people in the room, but it was electric. Those 300 people got their money's worth. We were in a small conference room and everyone left Dallas that weekend with a new passion for the business.

Kenny Troutt had the chance to meet and talk to everyone who attended that event. In 1991, Kenny was not the greatest public speaker, but it wasn't how he said it, it was what he said. He told the group that he was going to build the largest telecommunications company in the world and that we would all reap the benefits. I'm not sure Kenny even knew what all of that meant, but he got the crowd fired up. People would run through walls for Kenny. He was giving us an opportunity to fulfill our dreams and we were not going to waste it. Kenny hosted a pig roast in the parking lot of the home office as his way of thanking everyone for coming. I loved it, but couldn't wait to get home and start building my business.

Each year, it seemed, Excel experienced record growth and the attendance at Excelebration proved it. The convention moved from hotels in Dallas to the convention center to the American Airlines Arena where the Dallas Mavericks play. Pat and I also played a bigger role at Excelebration each year, from speaking at a breakout session to presenting an award to eventually hosting and emceeing the entire event. That was amazing! Speaking to more than 12,000 people at one time is something you never get used to.

It got to a point when the top income-earners could not even walk through the lobby of the hotels. We were stopped every two feet to shake someone's hand, sign an autograph or just talk to a rep who was trying to find the secret to building the business. Colleen and Cindy just went ahead without us. We would catch up to them a few hours later. If people wanted to talk to me, I wanted to talk to them. They were no different than me. They had goals and dreams just like I did, and I was going to give them my time. I loved to hear the stories of people from all over the country. Everyone had a story to tell and some of them moved me to tears.

The only thing better than listening to the reps at Excelebration was hearing from Kenny Troutt. His speech at the end of each convention was certainly the highlight of the weekend. He would speak with such passion that he moved all of us to action. That massive action made Excel a billion dollar company.

Kenny has a huge heart, but he is a ruthless business-man. To build a billion dollar company, you have to be. Still, he loved the reps and every decision he made, he made with them in mind.

During Excelebration, Kenny would invite the top 50 or so income-earners to his home. This was by invitation only and your name had to be on the list to get in. One year, a rep brought her boyfriend to Kenny's home and his name was not on the list. A cab was called, and the boyfriend was sent back to the hotel. Nobody messed with Kenny.

Kenny would provide transportation from the hotel and meet and greet all of us at his front door. Once again, it was a vision-stretching exercise. Kenny and Lisa's home was every-thing you expected it to be, and they were gracious hosts.

Pat and I became very good friends with Kenny. I learned so much and continue to learn from him today. I learned that to become successful, you need to be persistent. But you also need to be aware of what is working and what is not working. And you can't be afraid to make adjustments. Kenny would often call us to encourage us when we were down, and also congratulate us on a job well done.

Kenny was a master at selling the dream. He would tell us that it was time to take control of our time, our lives and our dreams. We decided to do just that.

In 1997, James W. Robinson wrote the book, *The Excel Phenomenon*. It was released at Excelebration that same year and millions of copies were sold. The reps bought hundreds at a time and used them as recruiting tools.

That year at Excelebration, I spent nearly my entire time autographing copies of the book. People would stop Pat and I and ask us to sign as many as 10 copies. It was crazy, but we were happy to do it if it helped them build their business. Lines 30 to 40 people deep would appear during breaks at the general session. I would joke with Pat about the celebrity status we had at Excelebration, even though we still had to take out the garbage at home.

Steve Smith always had fun at Excelebration. One year he arrived in his helicopter. He landed right there in the parking lot of the Anatole hotel. How does a person even get clearance for that? He invited a few of us guys to play golf with him, and he told Pat and me to meet him at the helicopter at 7 a.m. We thought he meant to meet him there with our car, so we could drive him to the course. Oh no, he was taking us to the golf course in his helicopter! We landed on the driving range.

At these types of events, I couldn't help but be inspired. I was surrounded by people who were living the lifestyle that I wanted. They were people just like me. I knew it was only a matter of time before I was living the life I was dreaming of.

The friendships that I have created in this business will last a lifetime. **Scott Pospichal** is one of those friends. We looked forward to seeing each other at Excelebration each year. We became great friends because Scott was just like Pat and me. We were all about the same age and we had the desire to make money. Scott struggled in the business just like we did.

Every night at Excelebration we would find a spot in the courtyard of the Anatole hotel and just laugh. We would tell stories until the early hours of the morning. Scott always had cigars for us during this time. I never smoked cigars unless I was with Scott and Pat at Excelebration. Jordan Adler would sometimes join us as well.

Everyone should have friends in their lives like Pat Hintze, Scott Pospichal and Jordan Adler. They are people that you don't need to talk to every day, but when you do, it feels like you just had lunch with them yesterday. They are people you can always count on. It doesn't matter what is going on in your life or if you need something, they are the friends who are there for you. I truly hope you have friends like that in your life.

Scott would often take Colleen and Cindy and just hang out with them all day when Pat and I were busy speaking or conducting a training class. We would meet them for lunch or dinner. They would always be waiting for us at the table and we would always be late. They all understood though. It was the nature of the business.

Even today, I look forward to the big events because of the people. Whether it's a national convention or a regional rally or even a super Saturday event, they are always special. The people who are attracted to this business want something more out of life. Some of them will not stop until they find whatever it is they are missing. It's always fun to be around people like that.

Those who understand how this business works know they need to help others. It is a team game. No one in this business has ever been successful by building on their own. It really is the complete opposite of corporate America. If you want to get to the top in corporate America, you often need to step on some people along the way.

For instance, if I worked for you, and you were my direct supervisor, and I told you that I was going to be vice president of the company someday, how much help would you really give me? Probably not very much because it might make you look bad if I pass you up.

But in this business, if I said to you, "I'm going to make more money than you ever dreamed of," and you really understood how the business works, you would say to me, "Great, I will help you every step of the way." That's because you get an override on whatever I do. As a result, it makes perfect sense for you to do whatever you can to help me achieve my goals. That's why more millionaires have been created in this industry than any other.

At big events, successful people are highlighted for two reasons. First, we want to congratulate them, and second, we want you to see that it's possible. It doesn't matter what your goals and dreams are, they are possible and often someone else has already achieved them. If one person has made over $1 million in one month, it is possible that you can, too.

That's why the big events are so important. In 23 years, I have only missed one major event and that was because my mother was very sick. I go to the events to be inspired. I don't care if it's my event, or if I'm emceeing the event, or if I organized the event, I'm there to find inspiration that helps me build my business.

Jordan Adler once said that for every person in your group who attends the national convention, you will grow your group by 100. So, if you had 10 people attend the event, your group should grow to more than 1,000 in the next few years.

Pat and I would start promoting the next big event on the day after the last big event. We always had people who would say they didn't need to go and hear all the hype, or that it was too expensive. I had one guy tell me he could not attend because he was going to miss his son's first birthday party. Now don't get me wrong, I am into family and birthday parties. But the big events will drive your business to a new level. The problem I had with his excuse was that his son was turning 1. He could have planned the party the next day or even the next week. I don't think his son would have known the difference. If that sounds cold to you, I'm sorry. I just feel that building a better future for your family is more important than a party that could have been rescheduled.

I worked my business around my family activities. When my kids were very young, I was gone all the time. Almost every night I was doing a business presentation or training somewhere. But my kids were in bed by 7:30 p.m. anyway.

I have often been asked if Colleen worked the business with me. My answer has always been yes. She had no idea how to give a business presentation or how to train a new rep; she was terrified of speaking in public. She never filled out a customer or new rep application, or answered any questions about the business. Those were not her roles in the business. On the other hand, I never knew when the kids had doctor or dentist appointments. I never had to keep track of the school activities. I had no idea when my children had a field trip or if they needed money for a project at school. I didn't have to know that information, Colleen did.

Colleen would give me plenty of notice when I needed to be somewhere with the kids. If I went on a field trip, I knew I had a chance to talk to other parents about the business. Life and work became one and the same for me. I tried to never miss my children's sporting events. I got their game schedules and put every game on my calendar, working my business around those games.

The partnership that Colleen and I had was just as important as the partnership that Pat and I had in the business. I had to create a balance and Colleen did that for me. She gave me the freedom to concentrate on building our future while she took care of the everyday living activities.

I did sacrifice some things when the kids were very little, but I made up for it as they got older. I was doing this business full-time before Megan, my oldest, was four years old. My kids have never seen their parents holding down a "real job." As the kids got into sports, I was able to coach their teams. When I was teaching school, people asked me all the time if I coached, but I never did because my objective was to quit my teaching position and work the business full-time. When I wasn't teaching, I was building the business.

I coached Emily's select basketball team from the time she was in fifth grade through eighth grade. That was an amazing time in my life. I had so much fun with those girls and we had a pretty good team. Our combined record for the four years was 101-49.

Scott Pospichal was an excellent basketball player and coach. He won a division two, national championship as a player and coached college basketball. I called Scott for basketball advice, and I had my fifth-grade girls running the same offense that Scott was using for his college athletes. I ran the same drills as he did. Some of my players' parents thought the offense was too complicated. I had no idea if it was or not. If Scott told me to run it, we ran it!

I would call Scott after each tournament and give him the play-by-play of how we fared. He would help me make adjustments for the next tournament. I swear, if Skype had been around then, I would have Skyped him into our huddles during timeouts to set up our plays.

During one game, we were tied 49-49 with 12 seconds to play. The opposing team was at the free-throw line shooting two shots. The girl missed the first, and when she missed the second, we called timeout to set up our final play. The game was very intense.

When the girls came over to the bench, they were all in tears. I just looked at them and asked, "What is wrong?" They all looked at me and said, "Nothing." To this day I still don't know what was wrong. I think they were just nervous. The first thing I told the girls was that we were going to win the game. I wanted to get their heads in the right place before they went back onto the court. I designed a play for Ashley, our star player. The play was called "Culvers." It was a play designed to give Ashley a chance to take the ball to the hoop. She would either make the shot or she would get fouled.

With 12 seconds left, we had plenty of time. Ashley walked the ball to the three-point line and yelled, "Culvers." Everyone cleared out and Ashley worked her magic. She drove down the lane and laid the ball over the rim as time expired. The place went nuts! Ashley was mobbed and we all ended up at Culvers for ice cream after the game.

I loved coaching Emily's team. We developed a special bond. After each game or practice we would talk on the way home about things we could have done differently. It wasn't always easy. She would often tell me to stop yelling at her friends. We still laugh about that today.

I was also able to coach my son Mike's baseball team as well. I could write an entire book on the difference between coaching boys and girls. Mike was a scrappy player and had great speed. When Mike got on base, he was always able to turn a single into a double or triple with his ability to steal bases. I don't think he ever got thrown out trying to steal.

Mike played second base. I would hit him ground balls for hours. Even in the winter, I would move the cars out of the garage and he would field ground balls in there. He also loved to play catcher. He was a little guy but very tough, and you need to be tough if you are going to be a catcher. We won a lot of games and created memories that will last a lifetime.

Megan's main sport was fast-pitch softball. She was a great hitter. Her select teams played tournaments all summer long. I did not coach her teams, but spent a lot of time on the bleachers watching her play.

If you've ever had kids that played sports, you understand what I mean by the term "bleacher time." I can't even begin to tell you how much time Colleen and I spent watching the kids play. I can count on one hand how many games I missed during those years. I loved watching the kids play sports. The reason I worked so hard at building the business and traveling all over the world was because it allowed me to create time for my true passion — my family.

What most people don't understand about building a business like this is that working very hard for a short time will allow you to have the time freedom that truly makes your life rich, later. Instead of just making a living, you will start living your life.

Scared Into Making Millions

Believe it or not, I have always been very shy. I never wanted to read out loud in school. I never wanted to participate in spelling bees. I never wanted to be at the front of the room or be the center of attention. In high school, I had to take a speech class. Most students enrolled as sophomores, but I waited until my senior year. I would lose sleep at night knowing I had to speak in front of my classmates the next day. In college, I again waited until my senior year to take a very basic speech class.

I earned a bachelor's degree in sociology at school, but had no idea what to do with it. That's why I ended up taking the job at the *Milwaukee Journal*. I really have no idea what I was thinking when I decided to go back to school and get my teaching certification. Remember, I was the one who was terrified to be at the front of the room, and I decided that's what I was going to do for a living! Somehow it seemed OK when I was in front of fifth graders, but when it came time to talk to adults about the business opportunity, that was a different story. I could tell those fifth graders anything. I couldn't get away with that with adults.

I remember thinking to myself that if I was going to make big money, I needed to be in front of the room. I found out that wasn't true, but it was a motivator for me to do it. The 10 most powerful two-letter words are: **If it is to be, it is up to me.** I learned that from **Dr. Jack Canfield** years ago. I love his teaching. His book *The Aladdin Factor* played a big role in my success. Jack has many different books to help with personal development. He is a valuable resource.

As I started showing the business opportunity to people, I realized that no one was going to give this to me. I needed to make it happen for myself. I had to step out of my comfort zone, since everything I wanted to achieve was outside of my comfort zone. That is exactly what I did.

We had a scripted business presentation, so I decided to memorize it. If I did the presentation word-for-word, I figured I wouldn't have any problems. I memorized the presentation and gave it over and over again. That simple practice led me to where I am in the business today. I didn't know it at the time, but memorizing the business presentation and reciting it over and over set the stage for my success.

I focused on the simplicity. Throughout my entire career, I have taught people to keep it simple. I have been doing the same training for over 23 years now. Repetition is the mother of all skills. Early on, I realized that the organization would grow if I could teach others a simple system that they could duplicate over and over. Today, that is still my goal. I have people who have been with me for more than 23 years. They can almost finish my sentences for me. My message is the same. It doesn't vary. If I changed my approach each week, or tried to entertain the reps each week, my group would never grow.

By keeping the message simple, I am always prepared, and the reps in my organization are able to learn the business building concepts quite easily. Remember the McDonald's theory? If you come to my business presentation or training, you know what you are going to get.

As it turns out, public speaking is the number one fear of most people. But you do not have to be a public speaker to build a business. You never have to be up in front of the room to make big money.

My friend **Phillip Eckart** was a perfect example of this. Phillip is one of the most successful networkers in the world. He was able to build a multimillion-dollar business without ever speaking in front of people. He did a lot of one-on-one presentations and used the system that was in place. He utilized the local meetings where other top income-earners did the presentations. He also used the DVD presentation and let the system do the work.

Today, I feel uncomfortable when I'm not in front of the room. I get very nervous just before I am supposed to speak, but as soon as I get in front of a group, calm comes over me. I feel at home in front of a crowd. That feeling took a long time to develop; it certainly did not happen overnight. It came from years of presenting the same message over and over.

People don't understand the work and dedication it takes from a mental point of view to build a successful organization. The hardest part for me was the mind game I had to play. I had to learn how to handle rejection. When my best friends and close family members turned me down, rejected what I had to offer, told me it would never work and not to quit my day job, it was tough. You have to be mentally tough!

It makes me feel sad that some of my best friends are not in my business today. I know they see the lifestyle I have and would probably love to live the same way, but for some reason, they don't see themselves as being capable of creating that kind of success. I believe their dreams are not big enough.

In my presentation, I show people how they can make more money in one month than they currently make in one year. For most people that's a pipe dream. They are not able to wrap their heads around the idea of that kind of success. But it's all around them. They love professional athletes, actors and performers, but they don't think that kind of success is a reality for them.

I'm going to assume that you were raised the same way that I was raised. When I was in school, my parents told me to go to high school and get a diploma, then go to college and get a degree, and then find a good job and work for the next 40 years of my life. That is exactly what I set out to do and I bet you did, too.

The problem was I could not make enough money to do the things I really wanted to do by building someone else's dream. I realized early on that when I was working for someone, I was doing just that. I could see it. It was plain as day. In fact, it smacked me right in the face. That sting is what led me to this industry and gave me the courage and tenacity to see the job through.

Most people are not like me, and I was trying to make them all think the same way I do. After a few years of banging my head against the wall, I decided to start sorting people out. I just wanted to find people like me. If I had to go through 100 people to find one like me, it was worth it.

Today, when people tell me no, it doesn't bother me. I understand the game. Each *no* I get brings me closer to a *yes*. Would I like to enroll every person I talk to? Of course, but that would only set me up for certain failure.

Bobby Buss has been one of my best friends since we were eight years old. We were college roommates, he stood up at my wedding, I love him to death, but he's not in my business. His wife Paula even worked for Pat and me for a while. I would love to have them in our business and have them enjoy the success we have had. There have been so many times I wanted to call Bobby and say, "Let's go to Mexico next week." Or "How about Vegas for the weekend?" But I knew he wouldn't be able to go because of money and time commitments.

I know I'm being selfish. I want Bobby to come on trips like that with me, but the truth is, Bobby might not want those things, or maybe he isn't willing to sacrifice what it takes to live that lifestyle. Maybe he feels like he just wouldn't be able to build it. It's not my job to figure that part out. It's my job to ask and then accept the answer. It's black and white. Yes or no. I'm in or I'm out. I can't force people to build a business. I can't force them to think the way I think. I can't force people to have a bigger vision. The only thing I can do is show them the potential and let them decide for themselves.

Once I learned all of this, it was like a 1,000-pound weight was lifted off my shoulders. I used to get so stressed while showing the business to someone because I was worried about whether or not they were going to sign up. I talked a lot of people into signing up for the business, but all of them quit soon after.

Les Brown once said, "A man convinced against his will is of the same opinion still." You don't need to talk anyone into the business. Either they see it or they don't. I know people think that I sign up everyone I talk to. That is not true. I just talk to more people. I sign up the same percentage of people that everyone else does. I bet I have collected more no's than most people. That's the secret. Go collect as many no's as you can and your life will completely change.

People don't understand how my family members can't be involved in my business after all of the success I've had. It's crazy isn't it? I don't understand it myself. My bother Bill signed up and quit. Colleen's sister Cathy and her husband Russ signed up twice and quit both times. Colleen's brother Mike signed up and quit. My sister Angie signed up and quit. Stop shaking your head. It's really OK. They just don't see what I still see today — an opportunity to create time and financial freedom.

My uncle Russ is a great guy. I love him very much but he didn't see the opportunity the same way I did. In fact, he didn't see it at all. When I showed my uncle Russ the business, he told me that it would never work. He told me that "pyramid deals like this" never work. He told me not to quit my job and not to expect to make any money.

After I left my teaching position, I again talked to my uncle Russ. He told me then that it would never last. So, his advice to me so far had been, "It will never work and it will never last." Now, after more than 23 successful years in the business, my uncle Russ tells me, "Now I'm too late."

To sum up his advice, "It will never work and it will never last; now I'm too late." Figure that one out! If you actually tried to figure out that logic, you would drive yourself insane.

When Colleen and I built our big house, I found myself apologizing for our success. When friends and family members would come over, they could not believe how beautiful it was. I would say things like, "Thanks, but try cleaning it." Or "It's nice, but the electric bill is $1,500 a month!" I don't know why I felt like I had to apologize for my success. They all saw the opportunity. They all had a chance to partake in the opportunity. They all had the exact same chance I did to get started. I'm not sure why I felt the way I did.

I'm telling you all of this because I want you to know that if you stick around long enough to have success in building a business like this, you will go through the same things I did. My story is not unique. Everyone who has experienced success in this profession has the same stories. The only difference between those who have made it and those who have not quite gotten there yet is longevity. If you persist, you will create the success you have been looking for and you will have the same stories I have been sharing with you.

Remember, success and failure are on the same road; success is just a little further down. Failure cannot handle persistence!

In The Spotlight

As Pat and I continued to build our business, doing the same presentation over and over, our organization continued to grow. As we became more successful, we became smarter. We were the ones people wanted to talk to. We had all of the bright ideas. We were written up in many books and magazines and won all kinds of awards. Pat and I would look at each other and just laugh! We would ask each other, "How did we get so smart?"

We weren't doing anything special. We found a system that worked and we stuck with it. If that makes us smart, I guess we'll accept that, but it's nothing that anyone else couldn't do as well.

Each week, we taught and trained other independent reps how to build their business. Everyone wanted to know the secret and we told them exactly what we were doing, and that if they applied the same techniques, they would enjoy the same success.

That reminds me of a story. There was an old pastor of a church in a small town in southeastern Wisconsin who, for five consecutive Sundays, preached the same sermon. After the fifth Sunday, the elders of the church got together and decided they needed to talk to the pastor about his sermons. The elders met with the pastor and said, "Pastor, do you realize that for the past five Sundays, you have been preaching the exact same sermon?"

The pastor replied, "Oh, you noticed." The elders said, "Yes, we noticed and everyone else has noticed as well." The pastor leaned back in his chair and said, "Good. I'm going to continue with that same sermon until you start to apply it."

I love that story because it applies so much to my business. If everyone would actually apply these simple principles on a daily basis, they would reach whatever goals they set for themselves.

For example, at my training sessions, I talk about creating a prospect list. A prospect list is the key to success. You can have the greatest financial opportunity in the world, but if you don't have anyone to share it with, it means nothing. I have reps in my organization who have heard my trainings for years and they still haven't made a prospect list; they wonder why they have struggled over the years.

I continued with the same "sermon" week after week, hoping people would apply the techniques. It's pretty easy to pick out the reps that did. They are the ones who are working the business full-time. They are the ones who are setting new goals and reaching them faster than ever. They are the ones who are living the lifestyle they have always dreamed about. It's available to anyone who is coachable and willing to do the work.

Our simple system of building the business had a major effect on hundreds of thousands of reps all over the world. As corporate trainers, Pat and I were able to travel all over the world and teach people how to reach a level of success they didn't know existed.

Emily and I learned how to surf on a trip to Hawaii. I was scheduled to do some training in Honolulu and Emily asked if she could come. On that trip we toured a number of Hawaiian Islands and even walked on hot lava. She still has her souvenirs on a shelf in her bedroom. The kids have been to Hawaii a number of times. Colleen took her first trip to the islands in December of 2012! Colleen has often joked that the kids have been all over the world while she has been stuck in Oconomowoc, Wisconsin. Colleen was only kidding —she knew what a great experience it would be for the kids to travel the world with their dad.

I've met wonderful people from all over the world and they are all similar. They might speak a different language, or eat different foods, or have different customs, but they all want the same thing — to live a good life and be happy. Life really is pretty simple if you think about it. If everyone would just treat others the way they would like to be treated, the world would be a much happier place.

I try to live my live my life by that motto every day. I always try to smile at others. I open doors for people, and it really does make a difference. When I was young, my mother always said, "It's better to give than it is to receive." I never understood that until I was an adult. You can give by just smiling, or opening doors, or laughing with others. Try it! Your life will change for the better.

I always try to make people feel good. I want to be remembered as someone who was always willing to listen and who was caring. I think I've done a pretty good job of that so far. Pat and I have never forgotten where we came from. We both understand that the only difference between us, standing at the front of the room, and those people listening to us, is time. We've just been doing it longer. We certainly don't have more talent or anything else that makes us special. We just never quit!

Pat and I have received many awards in this business. The two that we are most proud of are the Circle of Excellence Award and the Jay A. Smith Excellence in Training Award. We received the Circle of Excellence Award nine times. That award is very special because it comes from our peers. Thousands of independent reps from all over the world vote for people who demonstrate leadership qualities in helping others inside and outside of their organization.

What that award shows is that we don't see downlines. We only see people who want the same things we do, and we are willing to help regardless of downline affiliation. That has always come naturally to me. I've never thought there was any other way. It makes me happy knowing other people recognized it as well.

The Jay A. Smith Excellence in Training Award was also very special. Not only is it named after our good friend and mentor Jay Smith, but it also signifies that we can build an organization and teach others to do the same.

Only one person receives the Jay A. Smith Excellence in Training Award each year. Pat won it in 1997, and I won in 1999. I see the award on a shelf in my office every day, and it inspires me to keep working and helping everyone.

The inscription on the award reads, "The goal of many leaders is to get people to think more highly of the leader. The goal of a great leader is to help people think more highly of themselves."

I'm really not an awards kind of guy because I am more interested in seeing the people in my organization excel and achieve their goals. I get satisfaction when someone in my group gets an award or is recognized for a job well done. Still, the Jay A. Smith and Circle of Excellence awards prove to me that my heart was and still is in the right place. This business is all about helping others. If you can develop that mindset and get lost in other people's promotions, you will surpass all of your expectations and your life will be filled with abundance.

Life Lessons

As I grow older, I appreciate the phrase, "Life's too short," more and more every day. Life really is too short not to enjoy every waking minute. We all deserve to be happy. We were placed on this earth to not only enjoy our lives, but also enhance the lives of others.

I don't think I would have enjoyed my life as much as I have if I hadn't gotten involved in this business back in August of 1990. This business has given me not only financial freedom, but also time freedom, which is more important. You can make all the money in the world, but if you don't have the time to enjoy it, it means nothing.

When my son Mike was three years old, he was enrolled in half-day preschool. One morning, very early, Mike came into our bed and wedged himself between Colleen and me and said nothing. After a few minutes I heard a big sigh. I sat silent and just listened. A few minutes later, the sigh was louder. I turned to Mike and asked him what was wrong. He looked at me and said, "I have a test today."

Remember, he was in preschool. I said, "You have a test today? What kind of test do you have?"

He said, "Well, my teacher wants to see if I can zipper."

I asked him, "Can you do it?"

Mike said, "I don't know."

Let's set the stage here. This little guy was losing sleep because he was being tested on whether or not he could zip his jacket.

I said to Mike, "Do you want me to help you?"

He said, "Yeah!"

He jumped out of our bed, ran downstairs and grabbed his little Green Bay Packer jacket. For the next 45 minutes, I helped Mike learn how to zip up his jacket. If I had to go to work at a regular job, who would have helped Mike learn how to zip his zipper?

Life's too short not to help.

One year, my entire family came with me on a trip to Florida. Our first stop was Walt Disney World in Orlando. We had a great time of course — it was Disney World! We spent three days at the park before heading up to Daytona. I was scheduled to do a training class on a Saturday morning and then planned to hit the beach with my family in the afternoon. My training was to run from 9 a.m. to noon. Everything was going great until about 11:20 a.m. I saw Mike and Emily wandering around, staring at me. Emily was seven and Mike was five. All of a sudden, Mike led Emily down the aisle in the meeting room and headed right towards me. When they stood right next to me, I stopped, looked down and Mike said, "Dad, are you almost done or what?"

He was ready for the beach, the sea turtles, the sand castles and the s'mores. I simply turned to the 150 people in the audience who heard Mike's request and said, "This is why I do this business." I finished up before noon and we were on the beach by 1 p.m.

> *Life was way too short for Mike
> to listen to my training session.*

I was doing a business presentation at the home of one of my new reps. He did a great job of filling his home with guests. I bet we had 40 people in the room; 30 were looking at the business for the first time. I was super excited for him.

In those days, we used a flip chart to do the presentation. It was heavy; it measured two feet by four feet and had thick plywood backing. I got everything set up. It was perfect. I was ready to sign up a bunch of new reps that evening.

As I got into the presentation, the audience was playing right into my hands. They loved the concept and I was on fire! We were all laughing and talking about the possibilities that came with the opportunity.

My rep had just moved into his new home and it was beautiful. About halfway into the presentation, one of the legs of the tripod started to give way. From that moment on, everything was in slow motion. As the tripod collapsed, the flip chart slowly fell into the wall. The corner of my heavy chart and its wood backing went right into the newly constructed wall of the living room. And it stuck there!

The crowd gasped in amazement. I looked at the chart, I looked at the audience, I looked at my new rep, and then I tilted my head to match the flip chart and continued with the presentation! Everyone loved it and laughed out loud.

Life's too short to worry about a little hole in the drywall. Don't worry, I paid for the repair!

My workweek consisted of doing business presentations at 7:30 p.m., Monday through Thursday, in someone's home or at a hotel. I would do lunch meetings every Monday at 11:30 a.m. at the Midway Hotel in Brookfield, Wisconsin. I would meet anyone, anywhere, any other time if they could meet with me. And I did training classes every Saturday morning.

My friends who had "real jobs" would often call me on Friday and ask if I could play golf with them on Saturday. They knew my routine, but they would ask anyway. I would always tell them no because I had to help all of my new reps get started on Saturday morning.

One of my friends said to me, "Man, I wouldn't do what you do for nothing." (Isn't it a good thing I don't do it for nothing?)

I replied, "I can't play on Saturday, but I'm free Monday morning, or Tuesday, or Wednesday for that matter." I knew darn well he wasn't available to play during the week. His job was getting in the way!

Life's too short not to play golf on an empty golf course during the week.

Throughout this book, I have talked about the need to sort people out in order to build a networking business. It's just a matter of finding people. Everyone wants to find the next big income-earner, and trust me, those people are looking for you as hard as you are looking for them.

J. Paul Getty once had 47 millionaires working for him at the same time. A reporter asked, "How did you get 47 millionaires to come and work for you?" Getty laughed and replied, "They weren't millionaires when I hired them."

The reporter went on to ask, "How did you find the quality person it takes to become a millionaire?"

Getty said:

"You look for millionaires the same way you look for gold. When looking for gold, you don't stick your shovel in the ground and come up with a shovel full of gold. You stick your shovel in the ground and come up with a shovel full of dirt. But you expect the dirt. You discard it because you're not looking for the dirt you're looking for the gold. You know up front that if you are going to find gold, you are going to move a lot of dirt. If you are looking for the quality person it takes to become a millionaire, you are going to move a lot of people."

That's the challenge in this business. The gold is the 20 percenters. The gold is not easy to find, but it's out there. If this business was liedown easy, it would not be available to any of us. If gold was as plentiful as dirt, it would have no value. If brain surgery were easy, there wouldn't be any money in it. This business is just tough enough that it weeds out the people who don't want to do it, so there is more for those of us who do!

The 80 percenters will often bring you to the 20 percenters. It's not about you and what you do; it's about you and what you start. Once you get your business started with the right people, there is no way of stopping it.

Life's too short not to dig for gold.

I was sitting in my office back in June of 1997 when my phone rang. As I answered, a pleasant male voice on the other end of the line said, "Is Bill available?" I told him that he had the wrong number, but for some reason, I didn't want the conversation to end there. I asked what number he was trying to call. He told me the number and it wasn't even close to mine. We both kind of laughed and he said goodbye.

Before he hung up, I asked him where he was from and he told me Boston. I said I had some good friends who lived in New England and we talked about what a great city Boston was, and then the fact that I lived in the Milwaukee area — just small talk. That all took place in about two minutes.

Then I said, "You know, this might be crazy, but have you ever thought about starting your own business?"

His answer almost knocked me off my chair. He said, "I've been looking for something for the past six months."

I said, "We need to talk. I make a living showing people how they can start, own, and operate their own business, without giving up anything they currently do. Let me ask you this: How would you like to get paid every time someone made a long distance phone call?"

He said, "Are you serious?"

I said, "Yes!"

I explained how the opportunity worked and put together a package to send to him. (This was in the days before

147

the Internet.) I told him that he needed to get started at the highest level because I needed a person who could train others in the New England area. I mailed him all of the paperwork he needed to get started. The cost was $690. He said he would fill everything out and send it back to me.

I hung up the phone and said to myself, "No way! There is no way this guy is going to fill out everything necessary and send me a check for $690."

He filled out the independent rep and training application and sent it back to me two days later! I could not believe it. I called him to welcome him aboard. He asked if I would be willing to come to Boston for a few days to help him get started. Of course I was, and I asked him when would be a good time for me to come to Boston. I was talking to him on a Tuesday, and he said, "What are you doing on Thursday?"

I said I was busy. I wasn't, but I was not sure if this guy was for real yet. I told him I could come to Boston in two weeks, but he needed to get a bunch of people started before I could come out. I wanted him to prove to me he was serious about the business before I spent the time and money to fly out there. He agreed to have 10 to 20 people in his group within the next two weeks.

He made good on his promise. Two weeks later, as Colleen was driving me to the airport, she asked, "How do you know he's not some psycho killer?"

I said, "You know Colleen, I hadn't thought about that until right now. I'll be fine."

My new rep, Dave, was waiting for me at Boston's Logan airport, and we traveled to his apartment on Hanover Street. The thing I remember most about that ride from the airport was how crowded and narrow the streets of Boston looked.

We walked up the stairs to his second floor apartment and were greeted by 23 people who were ready to hear about the Excel opportunity for the first time! The flip chart was already set up and in place. All I had to do was start talking. We had a great meeting that night. The room was full of energy and people looking to make a positive change in their life. On Friday, we met a few people for lunch and held another meeting that night at the home of Dave's new rep.

On Saturday, we went to New Canaan, Connecticut, to meet a few more people. On Sunday, we had a training session and I trained 27 new reps, all of which had joined the business over the past three days. All of this was from a wrong number!

Life's too short not to answer the phone
and start asking a few questions.

Throughout the years, I have met some very interesting people from all walks of life. It did not matter to me what their background was — all they needed was a desire to improve their life. Some people signed up on the spot after seeing the presentation. Others had to "check the company out." Some people even told me they had all the money they needed and the opportunity was not right for them.

I have heard every objection imaginable:

"I don't have the time."

"I don't have the money."

"I don't want to make money off my friends."

"It's one of those pyramid deals."

I decided to have some fun with a guy who asked, "Is it one of those pyramid deals?"

I turned to him and said, "Yes it is, but we have a deal set up with the Attorney General's office. The Attorney General said that this program won't crash within the next three to five years, and in the next three to five years, we are going to be able to put between $3 and $4 million dollars into an off-shore bank account."

The guy just stared at me. I continued, "And when this thing finally does crash, we're only going to have to do six months in a minimum security prison."

He was stunned at what I was telling him. After a few seconds he turned to me and said, "Are you sure we're only going to have to do six months?" For some people, the more illegal and dangerous the opportunity is, the better!

Life's too short not to have a little fun with your prospects.

Roll With the Changes

When you do something for more than 23 years, you know there are bound to be changes. Some of those changes will be positive and some will be negative. I have always understood that Kenny Troutt needed to make changes for the betterment of the company and the reps. When other telecommunication companies lowered their rates, Kenny would counter with a new calling plan. When he announced the new rate structure at a regional conference or the national convention, the crowd would go crazy! I would just sit there and support the decision, knowing that the other reps didn't understand what had just happened. Their commissions were cut as well.

I wished the long-distance rates were a dollar per minute! My mom and dad would still be my customers. What most reps didn't understand was that Excel was not in competition with anyone. The business was all about relationships. For example, I prefer to do business with people who do business with me. If my dry cleaner or my insurance agent wasn't my customer, I would have found a new dry cleaner or insurance agent. I didn't care what the long-distance rate was, these people needed to be my customers because of our relationship. I always focused on the big picture and that was my next goal. I stayed in my lane. My job was not to question the policies the company enforced; my job was to build a business. I knew there had to be a good reason for every move the company made, and that included its sale.

Kenny built Excel to support his family and when he had the chance to sell it, he did. It was a great move for him, one of those business moves that will be talked about forever. I was so happy for him. He built Excel from the ground up, from a 900-square-foot office where he shared a desk. When he sold the company, he became a billionaire. I am very proud that I had a part in building the company, and that things turned out the way they did for Kenny.

At the time Kenny sold Excel, there was a lot of uncertainty. Many reps stopped building their business to see what was going to happen. I never did. I had a chance to talk to Kenny and he told me the company would continue to operate the same way it always had. That was all I needed to hear.

Think about it: Why would someone buy a billion dollar company as profitable as Excel was and start making changes? It didn't make any sense. With that thought in mind, I kept building my group. Everything seemed OK. The new owners loved the concept and loved the money they were making. Excel was even expanded internationally.

Kenny sold Excel to a Canadian telecom company with a large infrastructure, and the future looked good. I was excited about the move, and really happy for Kenny. I hated the fact that Kenny was not in charge anymore, but I felt he left us in good hands. I always believed in Kenny and still do to this day. He is a fantastic businessman and a great friend.

In less than two years, Excel was sold again to a Texas-based, dial around telecom company. That is where the train started to leave the tracks! I'm not sure if the new owners truly believed in network marketing. It seemed as if they were making changes to bring back a traditional business model.

That question was soon answered. All of the reps were notified that Excel would no longer be marketing its services through its current distribution channels, and that the compensation for the independent marketing directors would terminate on Friday. Wow!

Colleen and I closed on our new 13,000-square-foot home on Nov. 1, 2004, and realized we had already received our last commission check from Excel. That was not really a good day — we had some choices to make. We could either curse what had happened or embrace it. We decided to embrace it. We looked back over the past 14-plus years and were thankful for everything we had and for all the friends we had made.

The years I spent building my Excel business made up a chapter in my life that Hollywood could not have written. There were so many twists, so many turns, and so many life lessons learned. I would not trade a second of it! I met so many great people from all walks of life. The common bond among all of them was that they laughed, they were caring, and they had the dream of living a better life. Most of them did not choose Excel as their way of creating that better life, but that was OK. I walked away with friendships that will last forever.

In my years with Excel I made more money than most people make in 10 lifetimes. I saw many people making more in a month than they used to make in a year. The Excel opportunity changed the lives of thousands of people. I am proud to have played a small role in that positive change.

The day Excel closed its doors for good, I got a phone call from a very good friend, Annie Trajlinek. We'd been working Excel for many years together and I sponsored Annie in the business. When I said hello, she simply said, "What are you going to do?" I told her I wasn't sure I was going to do anything. My attitude was sort of, "been there, done that." Her advice at that time was another turning point in my life.

Annie said, "You are 40 years old. You are unemployable. You will never go to work for someone, but you have to do something. You need to see what Billy is doing."

I knew exactly who she meant when referring to "Billy." Bill had been in my Excel organization for a few years and built a fairly large group. He opened his first restaurant when he was still a teenager and had been an entrepreneur his entire life. He was a self-made millionaire. Bill had money but not time freedom. Annie had invited him to an Excel opportunity meeting and he heard my story. The time freedom was what Bill was looking for, and he immediately joined my business. After a few years, Bill left Excel to start his own MLM company, Financial Destination, Inc. (FDI).

When Excel closed its doors, FDI was about 18 months old. Bill had something pretty special in his hands, but it was just getting started. I told Annie to call Bill and have him come to Wisconsin and show me his business. This was on a

Friday afternoon and Bill, Annie, and a few other FDI reps were on my doorstep by 10 a.m. Monday morning.

I sat through a four-hour business presentation, soaking up everything Bill was telling me. The funny part about our meeting was that I didn't really care about the services Bill was selling. I knew that if he had been selling them for the past 18 months, and almost 5,000 people had joined his company, they must be great services. My whole concern was the four-hour business presentation! I thought, "If I have to give a four-hour presentation to get people interested, I'm out!" Bill and I still laugh about it today. I gathered all the information from the meeting and told Bill that I would let him know in a few days.

The next day I was on an airplane heading to San Francisco to meet with the owners of Shaklee, a billion-dollar health and wellness company. The people at Shaklee offered all the Excel reps the opportunity to join Shaklee and keep their downline in place. Bill told me that if I went to meet with Shaklee, they would wine and dine me to the point where I could not refuse their offer.

He was right about one thing — they took good care of us. They asked Tony Robbins to tell us how wonderful it was to be a part of this billion-dollar company. Everything was great. They even offered to pay us $10,000 per month, for one year, until our business was back on its feet.

How could Bill compete with that? Bill's company was a startup, and Shaklee was a 50-year-old, billion-dollar, established company. Still, Bill offered one advantage for me, and that was the fact that I didn't want to sell vitamins to my friends and family members.

I thought people who took nutritional supplements were crazy! I was always taught that if you ate properly, you would get all the nutrition you would ever need. Of course I was wrong, but I didn't know it at the time.

I went to San Francisco even though I knew FDI and Bill Andreoli were going to be my new home. I needed to hear what Shaklee had to say. They did not tell me what I wanted to hear. I was scheduled to film the new Shaklee/Excel business presentation the next day. I told Laura Collins, a vice president of Excel who came over to Shaklee, that she did not want me on that video. When she asked why, I said, "I can't afford to stay here." Her reaction confirmed my decision. She didn't say anything. She didn't try to talk me into staying. She gave me a hug, wished me well and walked away.

I told my business partner and friend Pat Hintze everything Bill had said about FDI and the opportunity there. We had been in business together for 14 and a half years, but that was no longer going to be the case. Pat decided to stay with Shaklee and is building a multimillion-dollar business there today. Dissolving that partnership was a very strange feeling, but let me tell you how great Pat Hintze is. He told me that if things did not work out with FDI, I could come back to Shaklee and we would again be business partners with a 50/50 split. Trust me, you need friends in your life like Pat. To this day we talk every week. We share ideas, training methods, and even contests. There were times that FDI and Shaklee were running the same promotions! I love Pat like a brother. Our journey together is far from over. We still have big plans that need to be turned into reality. One thing I learned about Pat was to never bet against him.

I called Bill from San Francisco to let him know that I was on board. He didn't believe me at first, but after a few minutes he came to his senses. I told him that I believed in him and his leadership ability, that I wanted to play a major role in building his company from the ground up, and that he could count on me.

Bill put together a great team. I felt like a kid on Christmas day. I couldn't wait to start building my team again. Bill had enough faith in me to give me a corporate title. He made me the vice president of training. I told him that he could give me any title he wanted to, but I also needed to be a rep. I felt that if I was going to tell people how to build a business, I needed to be in the trenches with them. I didn't want to look back. I wanted to create new stories, make new friends and help Bill build his company.

Over the next six years, I did exactly what I did the first 14 years with Excel. I kept everything simple and taught people that getting "no's" were actually OK. It's funny how the same old approach continued to work.

There were thousands of people who left the network marketing industry after Excel went away. I talked to hundreds of them who cursed the industry. I never understood that. Many of them were making more money than they could possibly make at their traditional job. Companies go out of business every day — not just MLM companies, but traditional companies as well.

This is an old cliché, but it's still true. It's not what you are dealt in life; it's how you handle it. I decided to rise to the occasion and take on a new challenge. I could have easily faded away, licked my wounds and felt sorry for myself for the rest of my life. That would have been the easy thing to do.

But the network marketing profession has not only changed my life, but has changed the lives of my family members for generations to come. There is no way I would leave this profession. If companies decide to leave me, fine, I will find another company. This profession works for those who work it. You are truly paid what you are worth. There is no limit to your income. You promote yourself and give yourself pay raises. It doesn't get any better than that.

My persistence over the past 20 years has paid off. I have had the privilege of helping hundreds of thousands of people reach their financial goals. It really is an amazing feeling to have people come up to you with tears in their eyes and tell you that you have changed their life. You can't put a price tag on that.

To Be Continued

Bill and his team at FDI built an impressive company that was starting to draw attention from industry leaders. Bill's "reps first" policy and his ability to develop relationships were a major factor in the success of FDI.

I was never on the inside at Excel as far as creating policy, developing new products or even putting events together. I normally just showed up and did my thing. At FDI that all changed. Bill was very open to my ideas and let me implement some business-building techniques and schedule events. You should be able to point to a few individuals who have made a positive impact on your life. Bill Andreoli is one of those people to me.

As I write these words, my journey continues. I have recently joined forces with Kody Bateman, the founder and

CEO of SendOutCards. I have never met such a creative and driven visionary. Even after 23-plus years in the networking industry, waking up every day feels fresh and new. I have so much more to accomplish. I have so many more stories to tell.

Life is full of challenges; overcoming them is rewarding. Can you imagine life without challenges? You would never feel a sense of triumph. Why do you think millions of people play sports at all different levels? It's the challenge. It's the thrill of victory. The real key in life is how you handle the agony of defeat. Some people crumble while others dig down deep, face defeat head on, and win the next battle.

I look at my life as a series of battles — some friendly, some not. But in either case, I will never give up, quit, or back down. Whatever life has in store for me, I accept it and deal with it. These changes and challenges include health, relationships, friends, jobs, investment opportunities, and anything else you can think of.

Life is way too short to be unhappy or to throw in the towel. I hate the word "retire." Why don't people just use the word "die" instead? To me, retire means to give up, quit, and stop. Is that what we all have to look forward to? Not me, and I hope not you.

I feel that I have a purpose on this planet and every day I look at the blueprint that was designed for me and try to execute the best plan possible, knowing darn well the plan may change tomorrow. But I'm ready for it. I am ready for anything life throws at me. That has been the key to my success. God will never throw something at me, or you, that we can't handle. I wanted to quit this business thousands of times. My friends, my family, and my goals are what kept me going.

I can't wait to tell you the rest of the story. It's being written this very second. I still need to share how I made millions of dollars in this industry, and how I took a brand new rep, who was excited to get started, and taught that person my simple system. By just doing a few simple things over and over, it can lead to great wealth. My system is not learning a hundred different techniques and applying them once. My system is learning a few techniques and applying them hundreds of times. As I've said many times before, repetition is the mother of all skill. You certainly don't need any talent to be successful, you just need the desire to be better, and a Les Brown "It ain't over until I win" attitude!

My simple system — I can't wait to tell you all about it!

Emily Schulz

Growing up, I never really knew exactly what my dad did or how to explain it to people when they asked. I just remember telling people, "He travels on the weekends to show people how to start their own business." I still sometimes use that line today. He did travel on the weekends, but still managed to be my basketball coach and was able to attend all of our weekend tournaments. I'm still not sure how that worked out.

I have always thought that my dad's job was the coolest thing, and I really do enjoy watching him give business presentations. As most people would agree, he is really good at it! It amazes me how comfortable he is on a stage because I cannot give a presentation in front of my 30-person class without shaking.

My dad is probably the friendliest person you could meet, and just after meeting him, you walk away with a feeling like you have been lifelong friends. I remember being embarrassed going through the McDonald's drive-through with him because he would greet the cashier by her first name, "Hi Lisa, how is it going?"

Because my parents worked from home, I never had to worry about finding a ride to a friend's house, going to a babysitter's house after school, or not having a great dinner every night because my Mom was too tired. She was so involved in our elementary school, and I never hesitated calling her if I forgot an assignment at home.

Having her constantly available to help with homework and chauffeur us three kids around was just what I expected and what I thought was normal. I am now able to see how lucky I was to have my mom at my beck and call on a daily basis. This situation worked for our family because my dad was secure in his job and enjoyed what he did. My mom has told me multiple times that my personality is very similar to my dad's. For example, I get really excited and enthusiastic about big, maybe sometimes unrealistic, ideas. My dad and I have had multiple conversations in detail about starting our own restaurant, golf course, and even hotel. Big ideas and having huge goals is something we both enjoy talking and fantasizing about. I like brainstorming new ideas about businesses, learning about his company, and traveling with him.

I also really love money! I remember being in fifth grade, and waking up early before school to check the stock market. I finally convinced my dad to let me buy stock in Kimberly Clark, and I ended up making $700.

Since then, I babysat, and babysat, and babysat trying to earn money. Every time I got paid, I would hand my wad of dollar bills to my mom to immediately deposit in the bank. I remember once, Megan bought a laptop, my brother Mike bought a ton of electric airplane toys, and I chose to just keep my money in the bank, even at age 10! My habit of saving money definitely came from my dad. Even though he was making a lot of money and had a good career, I never felt like I was spoiled and had tons of extra unnecessary things. This is something I am grateful for; my parents have taught me to be very responsible with my money.

Growing up in a family where my parents were able to set their own schedule and work from home was something very special. They both worked very hard, but they had the time freedom that most people don't enjoy. The value of having time freedom is something I will achieve someday as well.

Megan Schulz

I was probably around 8 years old before I realized that most people's parents went to work every day. I remember being at a friend's house, on a weekday when we didn't have school, and wondering where her dad was, only to find out that he actually had to go in to an office every day. This was a revelation to me, coming from a household where my dad worked from home.

I loved the fact that I was able to have both of my parents at home every day. Although my dad had various meetings and had to travel at times, for the most part having both parents so present in my life was a great way to grow up. Not only was I blessed to have two very present parents, but I also always had everything I ever wanted, from swimming in the pool or the lake all summer, to trips to Florida, Mexico, and the Dominican Republic, getting a car when I turned 16, and leaving college debt-free. I feel so lucky that I was able to have all of these things and still have both parents as a constant presence in my life.

I love that my dad has always been his own boss and I love everything that his business has been able to provide for me over the past 24 years.

Mike Schulz

Growing up, the question "So what do your parents do?" was always a tough one for me. My go-to answer when describing my dad's job was usually along the lines of, "He owns his own business," or "network marketing," but to be honest, I had no idea what I was actually saying. I just knew that my dad's job was pretty unique and gave me opportunities that most other kids didn't have. I was, and still am, damn proud of him for that. I've been lucky enough to have the opportunity to travel all over the world, have access to education without having to worry about student loans, and grow up not having to worry about money.

I was the only one of my friends whose dad worked from home. For the longest time, all I knew was that my dad set his own hours, didn't answer to any boss, and traveled all over the country giving speeches. But even with all that traveling, I never once recall a moment where I thought my dad was inaccessible. Having both of my parents around for all of the biggest moments in my life was huge. Rarely would my dad miss a high school soccer game because he had to work or stay late at the office, like so many of my teammate's parents.

Having parents who never needed to clock in for overtime pay has made me very grateful and appreciative of what I have today. It's the hard work of my dad that motivates me to do more with my life than just go through the motions and settle for a 9-to-5 job with a wife, 2.5 kids, a picket fence and a dog.